40 DAYS TO
Complete God
CONFIDENCE

40 Stories Illustrate the Liberating Words
of Assurance from 1 John 5:13–15

40 DAYS TO
Complete God
CONFIDENCE

SUSIE SHELLENBERGER

An Imprint of Barbour Publishing, Inc.

Print ISBN 978-1-63058-378-1

eBook Editions:
Adobe Digital Edition (.epub) 978-1-63409-621-8
Kindle and MobiPocket Edition (.prc) 978-1-63409-622-5

The authors are represented by and this book is published in association with the literary agency of WordServe Literary Group, Ltd., www.wordserveliterary.com.

Published by goTandem, an imprint of Barbour Publishing, Inc., P.O. Box 719, Uhrichsville, Ohio 44683, www.barbourbooks.com

Our mission is to publish and distribute inspirational products offering exceptional value and biblical encouragement to the masses.

Member of the
Evangelical Christian
Publishers Association

Printed in the United States of America.

To Stephane Shellenberger.
You are the sister I always wanted.
Thank you for living *God confidence every day.*
I love you.
—SUSIE

Contents

GOD CONFIDENCE IS
REAL CONFIDENCE

DAY 1

Who Is God?

"God is not human, that he should lie, not a human being, that he should change his mind. Does he speak and then not act? Does he promise and not fulfill?"
NUMBERS 23:19

It's hard to be confident about someone we don't know. So the first step in becoming confident in God is getting to know Him.

Be assured from the above scripture that God isn't wishy-washy or deceitful. He is trustworthy. The more we trust someone, the more confidence we have in that person.

God is your *Creator* (see Isaiah 40:28)—you can relax knowing He understands how you're wired, because He did the wiring. He knows about the aches and pains, and He gets it that sometimes you just need to stay in bed a little longer.

God is your *Defender* (see Psalm 68:5). When you're facing opposition, know that He has your back and will handle your enemies. What's your responsibility? To rest in His peace.

Need guidance? He is your *lamp* (see Psalm 119:105). He will light the pathway before you so you won't stumble through the dark areas of life.

Psalm 18:2 promises that God is your *Rock* and your

Fortress. When you need to hide from the world, let out a huge sigh and simply rest in His arms.

God is a God of *love* (see John 3:16). Love defines Him. He willingly died for your sins. (More about that tomorrow.) There's absolutely nothing you can do that will make Him stop loving you. He will *always* love you. Again, it's who He is.

There's also nothing you can do that will make God love you any more than He does right now. He loves you intimately. Ultimately. Supremely. There's no earning it, and there's no deserving it. None of us will ever measure up to it. But we can thank Him for His supreme love by obeying Him (see John 14:23). Living a life of obedience to God delights Him.

God is also *forever* (see Psalm 102:12). That means you don't need to worry about Him leaving, dying, or moving. You can count on Him. He is *righteous* (see Psalm 145:17). And One who is righteous is trustworthy, dependable, and loyal. He is not going to leave you.

Need grace? We all do! And God is full of it. He is *gracious* (see Romans 3:24). What exactly is grace? It's favor, goodwill, and blessing. God delights in giving you grace! But it doesn't stop there.

He is also *merciful* (see Luke 6:36). Mercy is undeserved grace. It's the policeman who writes you a warning instead of a ticket—even though you were speeding. Mercy is the judge who puts you on probation instead of behind bars—even though you're guilty.

Mercy is God forgiving your sins and even sending His Son to pay the penalty for you. What a God! And as you get to know Him intimately, you'll become confident and rock solid in your relationship with Him.

So let's talk about getting to know God intimately. Have you realized that He wants to be your salvation? Here's the proof: "Surely God is my salvation; I will trust and not be afraid" (Isaiah 12:2).

Someone who is willing to die for you is certainly someone you can be confident in. Fact: If you were the only person on the entire earth, God still would have sent His only Son, Jesus Christ, to die on the cross for your sins. *That's love.* That's a God in whom you can have complete confidence.

Christ died on the cross for you so you could experience salvation—forgiveness for your sins. That's right—you were born with sin. But you're not the only one. The Bible says that all of us have sinned (see Romans 3:23). We've all fallen short of God's perfect standard.

Problem: God is perfect, and His kingdom is perfect. He loves His children, but He can't allow sin to exist in heaven. He could force us to seek forgiveness for our sins, but that wouldn't be true love. God is not a puppeteer. He has no interest in controlling your decisions. He wants you to follow Him because you love Him.

God demonstrated His love for us while we were still sinners. He didn't wait until we got our act together. While we were steeped in sin, His Son willingly went to the cross so that we could experience salvation—forgiveness for our sins.

Christ was a perfect sacrifice; He had never sinned. He was pure, yet He took on our sins as His own so we could experience forgiveness from God. What a gift! But the gift isn't ours until we actually accept it. How do we do that? It begins with a prayer.

Right now—at the very beginning of this book—while you're yearning to develop complete God confidence is the perfect time to begin a relationship with God. Please remember that knowing *about* God isn't the same as having a genuine, in-depth, growing *relationship* with Him. If you'd like to experience salvation—having your sins forgiven—you can pray this prayer.

These are not magic words. You can rewrite this and use your own words. But if you pray and truly mean it, salvation is yours (see Ephesians 2:8).

Dear Jesus, I believe You are the Son of God and that You willingly died for my sins. This is mind boggling. I'm so sorry that I've disobeyed You and have tried to run my own life. I understand that You want to guide me and help me live in obedience to You.

Will You forgive me, Jesus? Right now I'm choosing to place my faith in You. I commit my life to You. Thank You so much for granting me salvation right now. Thank

You for the forgiveness of my sins.

I love You, Jesus. I'm excited about living the rest of my life for You. Amen.

DAY 2

A Blind Man Gets
Twenty-Twenty Vision

*[Bartimaeus] began to shout, "Jesus,
Son of David, have mercy on me!"*
MARK 10:47

Jesus and His disciples were on their way to Jericho. A huge crowd was following. They were still outside the city limits, but the scene had already become frenetic. Possibly a few hundred had gathered. Vendors lined the streets. Children played noisily, running back and forth across the pathway in front of Jesus. Mothers thronged His presence with a variety of requests:

"Jesus, please heal my daughter. Her headaches—"

"Master, my son's leg is twisted. He was born this way."

"This will only take a moment. Please! Can You stop and touch my father? His high fever hasn't broken, and we're afraid."

Above all the chaos, a voice from one who had been ostracized for years called out, "Jesus! Son of David! I need mercy. I need help. Something's not right."

To bring that much attention to himself—when he was already considered an outcast—demonstrated that even though he didn't know Jesus personally, he had a lot of confidence in Him. This blind man had heard of Jesus. Perhaps he'd received word of the miracles Jesus had done. Maybe he knew of the claims Jesus made—that He was the Son of God.

All the blind man knew for sure was that he needed help. No one else had been able to give it to him. His life had been reduced to begging from travelers entering the city of Jericho. The city folks were embarrassed by him. In fact, they were trying to hush him. They didn't want Jesus—the local celebrity—to know they had this kind of riffraff outside their city gates.

But instead of hushing, the blind man yelled louder. "Jesus! I need mercy! I need help!" What confidence. What boldness. What desperation.

He was demonstrating a genuine spiritual desperation. He was so desperate to have a genuine encounter with Jesus that he was willing to do anything to get it. How God loves it when we're spiritually desperate for Him. How He rejoices when we yearn for intimacy with Him.

The blind man knew his life wouldn't get better on his own. Maybe you, too, have come to that conclusion. You may be able to make your life better temporarily, but for significant change that will last forever, you know you need the kind of help that can come only from God. The changes He initiates are good over the long haul. His help lasts forever.

It would be a smart guess to assume the blind man had tried everything else. But nothing significant or life changing had occurred for him. Maybe you can relate.

"Jesus, I need help."

To make that statement requires boldness. The statement itself reflects faith, because you wouldn't say it unless you believe the hearer has the ability to offer the help you need.

The blind man had complete God confidence.

And Jesus stopped.

Think of all that was vying for attention from the Son of God that day: the smell of freshly baked bread being sold by vendors, the sound of sizzling fish frying in pans, children squealing, a few chickens running loose across the road, a few cows being led to the other side of the road. But what stopped the Son of God? The humble prayer of a man with a disability.

Wow. What a beautiful demonstration of the power of prayer.

What a dynamic illustration of God's concern regarding our needs.

Did the blind man give his life to Jesus? Yes. We can tell by the way he addressed Jesus: "Lord," he replied (Mark 10:51 KJV).

Lord.

Not Teacher. Or Prophet. Or Good Man. Or Friend. Or Dude. *Lord.*

In that one word, the blind man said all this: "I believe You are who You claim to be—the Son of God, the Messiah—and that You can forgive my sins. I want that! And I'm placing my faith in You right now. I want to live for You and obey You and live with You forever in heaven. Will You forgive my sins? And I'd sure love to see!"

Christ's response: "Your faith has healed you. Begin seeing."

Instantly the blind man could see and began praising God, and all who saw his healing praised God, too.

How was his God confidence evidenced? Through boldness (by calling out to Christ). Through desperation (by calling out to Christ in spite of the crowd pressuring him to be silent). Through humility (by admitting that he needed help).

A blind man's life was changed forever when he demonstrated his confidence in God. His life had been reduced to begging. He had no status in society. He was treated as a reject. Yet one genuine encounter with Christ gave him healing, hope, purpose, a place in society, forgiveness, and new life.

How can you demonstrate your God confidence today? Will you ask Him to help you develop a spiritual desperation for intimacy with Him?

DAY 3

Ready, Set. . .Grow!

But grow in the grace and knowledge of our Lord and
Savior Jesus Christ. To him be glory both now and forever!
2 PETER 3:18

Once you have an actual relationship with Christ, you can begin the amazing adventure of growing closer to Him—and this is how your complete confidence in God will develop. Growing close to someone takes time, right? Just like establishing a new friendship with anyone, you'll want to spend time with Him, communicate with Him, and simply learn to know Him on a deeper level.

It's actually every Christian's responsibility to grow closer to God. Here are the instructions: "And now just as you trusted Christ to save you, trust him, too, for each day's problems; live in vital union with him. Let your roots grow down into him and draw up nourishment from him. See that you go on growing in the Lord, and become strong and vigorous" (Colossians 2:6–7 TLB).

Remember our goal is complete God confidence. We establish that by becoming intimate with Him. And we enter into intimacy through His Word and through prayer. We'll discover—using the Bible as our guide—how to grow closer to Him and how to solidify our faith.

At the beginning of a relationship with Christ, our faith is small. And that's okay. After all, Jesus said it only takes a little bit of faith to experience salvation. But as we grow in Him, our faith expands and our confidence in Him deepens greatly.

Another thing we can do to enhance our spiritual growth is to find a church and get involved. The advantages of corporate worship are multifaceted. We all need accountability, and by showing up and getting involved in a local church, we enter into vulnerability with those around us.

By getting involved in a church, we also develop a bigger worldview—we realize that life is not simply about us, and we become more global minded. We begin to pray for international ministries, support missionaries, and become aware of Christians who are persecuted for their faith.

We can also learn to study and understand the Bible through gifted church leaders and in Bible study groups and Sunday school classes. Through the local church, we learn to carry one another's burdens (see Galatians 6:2) and share the excitement of God answering prayer in one another's lives.

Corporate worship also serves as a vehicle to bring us directly into the presence of God. Surrounding ourselves with praise music, learning new songs, hearing the testimonies of others, and lifting our spirits collectively to Him brings us right to His feet. He inhabits our praise. He delights in it (see Psalm 22:3). Where and how can we learn to praise God? In church.

Trisha is a nurse at a local hospital in my city. When she told me she was a Christian, I responded in excitement and told her she was in a prime place to reflect Christ to those filled with hurt who surrounded her. We continued our conversation, and when I asked her which church in town she attended, she told me she didn't go to church and had no desire to attend.

"How do you grow in your faith?" I asked.

"What do you mean?" she said.

"What are some things you're doing to grow closer to Christ without church?"

She thought for a few minutes then finally said, "Well, I listen to the Christian radio station on the way to work every day."

Faith-based music is great. I love it! But if that's the only spiritual nourishment we get, we'll soon become malnourished. We need more. We need a balanced diet of godly influences in our lives, and many of those come from church.

Spiritual growth is our personal responsibility. Let's look at what the apostle Paul said in Colossians 2:7: "See that you go on growing in the Lord, and become strong and vigorous in the truth you were taught" (TLB).

Notice the personal instruction from the above verse. Think back to your childhood. You may recall phrases such as "Clean your room," "Pick up your clothes," and "Brush your teeth." Your parents wanted you to learn that these things were your responsibilities. As you grew older, you no longer had to be reminded of these things, because they became good habits that simply transitioned into your lifestyle.

It works the same way spiritually. Christ desires that His disciples become mature in their faith. This means we need to discipline ourselves in spiritual growth practices. If you'll read the Bible at least *one minute* every day, it will eventually transition into a good habit that will become easy to do.

It's the same with prayer. Learn to pray about everything. Make talking to God throughout your day a part of your lifestyle. Don't relegate prayer to something you do only in the morning, before meals, or as you fall into bed at night. Learn to live in the presence of God 24-7 so that even the thought of being outside His presence would make you nauseous.

And of course, this same principle works with church attendance and involvement. When you're not committed to attending every Sunday, it's very easy to skip. Warm weather is an open invitation to the lake, and cold weather lures you to stay inside by the fire. But when you turn church attendance into an actual commitment, and when you get involved with a ministry in the church, it becomes easy to show up each week.

Though it's our personal responsibility to discipline ourselves with spiritual growth practices (Bible reading, church ministry, scripture memorization, meditation on the things of God, prayer, sharing our faith, etc.), the Holy Spirit guides and helps us in our actual spiritual growth.

As you draw closer to Christ, your confidence in Him will soar! Your faith will deepen. You will begin seeing Him work *in* your life and *through* your life. And you will also become more and more like Him.

DAY 4

Complete God Confidence

*Trust in the LORD with all your heart and lean not
on your own understanding; in all your ways submit
to him, and he will make your paths straight.*
PROVERBS 3:5–6

It's easy to exercise our confidence in God when things are going well, isn't it? The promotion came through, the car repair didn't cost as much as you estimated, you got two for one without even knowing about the sale, your name was drawn as first-place winner in the radio contest, you have money in your checking *and* savings accounts. . . .

At this point, it's easy to say, "God is faithful. I trust Him completely." But the most exciting thing about being in relationship with God is that He never changes! In fact, according to James 1:17, He doesn't even shift like a shadow. He is constant. Hebrews 12:28 tells us His entire kingdom can't even be shaken!

This is good news. It means you can count on God to remain faithful when others aren't. When you don't get the promotion, when your job is phased out, when a loved one dies, when your check bounces, God still remains true. You can continue to have unwavering faith in an unchanging God.

Regardless of the uncertainties, struggles, and disappointments you experience in life, your one true source of hope and assurance remains the same: Jesus Christ. You *can* have complete God confidence in the One who has promised to meet your needs no matter how hopeless things may look.

We don't always understand His ways. But a mature Christian is not someone who understands; it's one who accepts God's ways without understanding. Spiritual maturity is saying, "Father, I don't know what's happening. It seems as though my world is falling apart. I admit it; I'm scared. But You've never let me down in the past—and because You don't change, I know You won't let me down now. Help me to continue to trust You though I can't see You working. Help me to accept Your ways without understanding them. I can't see a light at the end of this tunnel, but I believe it's there. Strengthen my faith each day, Father."

That's a God-confident attitude. You may not always *feel* confident in God, but you can trust without feeling. Faith goes much deeper than emotion. Allow God to stretch your faith.

Complete God confidence is developed through a genuine relationship with Christ, spiritual growth in Christ, and trials. Think of trials as an opportunity to deepen your faith so that even in the darkest night you can still have complete God confidence!

Let's look at 1 John 5:13: "I write these things to you who

believe in the name of the Son of God so that you may know that you have eternal life" (NIV).

Your health may fail, the job may be terminated, and loved ones may leave. . .but you can have complete God confidence in the *fact* that no one can take away your relationship with Christ! This is eternal. The Bible tells us that heaven and earth will someday pass away (because God will make new heavens and a new earth), but our relationship with Him can be unshakable.

The flowers will fade, earthly promises are only temporary, and the most beautiful wonders of the world will disappear, but your relationship with God can't be demolished, removed, or snatched away. Doesn't it make sense to place all your confidence in the One who holds you forever?

Doug lost his job with a company he'd been with for twenty years. Because of the economy, they needed to down-size and Doug's department was terminated. Though Doug was devastated, he clung tightly to his faith in God.

"Sure, I'm scared," he said. "But deep inside I know God has my back. I have no idea if I'll be staying here or if I'll need to sell my house and move. I don't have a clue what I'll be doing next, but I know for a fact that God has always met my needs. He won't desert me. Yes, I've lost my job, a steady income, and my friends from work, but I have to believe that God has something even more exciting for me ahead. I hope that doesn't sound cocky. I'm still scared. There's a

Grand Canyon–sized lump in my throat, but I really do have complete confidence in my heavenly Father."

God confidence is *real* confidence!

DAY 5

Bond Servant

*Paul, a servant of Christ Jesus, called to be an
apostle and set apart for the gospel of God.*
Romans 1:1

Oftentimes when the apostle Paul begins a letter in the
New Testament, he announces himself as "Paul, a servant of
Christ Jesus." He does this in his letter to the Romans, and
he also does it in his letter to the Philippians and to Titus.

But Paul isn't the only one who does this. Peter identifies
himself the same way as he begins his second letter, and
James and Jude do the same thing in their letters.

In this context, they're using the word *servant* as in
being a *bond servant*—sometimes referred to as a *bond slave*.
What is a bond servant?

It was rare, but sometimes a slave would have a wonderful
master who loved and respected him. The kind master
treated his slave so well that even after the slave gained his
freedom, he chose to remain with the master. He trusted
him and knew he was safe with the master, and he would
rather belong to him and be provided for than risk being set
free and captured by someone who would abuse him and
treat him cruelly.

So when a slave made the decision to remain with his master, he was called a bond servant. The master would have the slave stand against the doorpost and would drive an awl through the ear of the slave. This would mark him forever as belonging to this specific master.

Again, this was something the slave chose. He had such confidence in his master that it was easy to trust him with his life. He knew his master would continue to provide for him and would love him as his own family. The awl's marking would prove to the world who owned him. He could never be stolen. This gave the slave tremendous security and a sense of belonging.

Paul, Peter, James, and Jude also referred to themselves—in the letters they wrote—as Christ's bond servants. By doing so, they were exhibiting complete God confidence in Christ to take care of them, meet their needs, and preserve them through eternity.

We, too, can become bond servants to Jesus Christ. Thankfully, we don't need to have an awl driven through our ear. We have another sign or mark that identifies us as belonging to Christ. We have the Holy Spirit. He identifies us. He guides us. He teaches us. And the Holy Spirit draws us into deeper intimacy with God Himself.

By thinking of ourselves as bond servants, we're immediately proclaiming that we have complete confidence in God to provide for us, save us, strengthen us, and keep us for eternity.

Did you know that God has placed a seal of ownership on those who trust Him?

"Now it is God who makes both us and you stand firm in Christ. He anointed us, set his seal of ownership on us, and put his Spirit in our hearts as a deposit, guaranteeing what is to come" (2 Corinthians 1:21–22).

Imagine that when you placed your faith in Christ and became a Christian, you were branded with His name on your forehead. *Ouch!* Not only would that be extremely painful, but it would also cause quite a stir among your family and friends.

But keep imagining with me. . . . It would also make your life easier. *How?* you may be thinking. Well, if the name *Jesus* was actually branded into your skin, you could easily use that mark on your forehead as a measuring standard for everything in your life. For example, you may be wondering about a questionable business deal. It's not outright evil, but you feel uneasy about it. Standing in front of a full-length mirror, you hold the file folder with the business deal up to your forehead. No, it doesn't go with the mark on your skin. Better not do it.

Should I see this movie everyone is raving about? Holding up the mirror to your forehead, you can clearly see it's a movie that doesn't go against the character of God. It actually complements the mark on your skin. It's written with family values and has a good message. Sure, go see it!

Wouldn't that make life easier? In a sense, we *do* have that brand on us. It's not actually on our foreheads; it's all over our lives. Hopefully, it's becoming part of your very lifestyle. That mark is the Holy Spirit. Today's scripture tells us the Spirit is our branding—proof that we belong to Christ. But instead of having to hold every decision up to our forehead in front of a mirror, we can depend on the Holy Spirit to guide us through our hearts.

As we pray about our decisions, we can trust Him to guide us in making wise choices that reflect God's character instead of accepting things in our lives that go against His character. But the scripture also says that the Holy Spirit in our hearts is simply a deposit—a guarantee—that we're getting more!

What more will we get? Besides eternal life with Christ, we'll also get the fruit of the Spirit as outlined in Galatians 5:22–23. As we continue to align our decisions and ourselves with Christ, the fruit of the Spirit will begin to manifest itself in our lives. As it does, our confidence in God will continue to grow.

As you make decisions about your life, your loved ones, your recreational activities, your habits, your use of money, imagine holding these decisions next to the name of Jesus. The Holy Spirit—God's branding on your life—will guide you into making wise choices that reflect the fact that you belong to Him.

GOD CONFIDENCE CHANGES US

DAY 6
On a Mission

*My God will meet all your needs according
to the riches of his glory in Christ Jesus.*
PHILIPPIANS 4:19

I was sixteen years old and headed to the school bus stop on a crisp, cool Wednesday morning. As I walked up the hill to cross the street and wait on the corner, I continued the prayer I'd been praying for the last two weeks. "Dear Jesus, tonight's the deadline. I have to turn the money in tonight if I'm going on the mission trip with the youth group between Christmas and New Year's. You know how badly I want to go. But we just don't have the money. I'm not asking for something frivolous. This is a *good* thing I'm seeking. I believe it's in line with Your will. And because You're all-powerful, I know You can provide the money I need if You want me to go. I'm trusting You."

I was part of a large high school youth group. The sophomore class participated in a mission trip within our state. The junior class would go out of state. And the senior class would go out of the country. A year earlier, I had participated in the sophomore in-state trip, and it had bolstered my confidence in serving Christ. I saw Him work through our group of ordinary students, and it was exciting.

Now, as a high school junior, I longed to go on the mission trip to Uvalde, Texas. Our group from Oklahoma would spend a week in a small, seventy-member church and would immerse ourselves in painting and beautifying it. We'd also canvas the area, inviting everyone we could to the special services we'd be holding. We had already learned to share our faith and pray with others, so this would be an exciting week.

But as much as I longed to go, I didn't have the money, and my family didn't have the extra funds to send me. But they helped me pray, and we believed that if God wanted me to participate, He would surely provide exactly what I needed.

So once again, climbing the hill to cross the street and stand on the corner to wait for the school bus, I poured my heart out to God. Then I decided to thank Him ahead of time for providing what I needed. After I climbed off the bus that afternoon and walked down the hill to my house, I absentmindedly collected the mail from our mailbox and placed it on the kitchen table. As I did, I noticed an envelope addressed to me. I opened it to find a check for some work I had done months earlier. Yes! It was just what I needed for the mission trip.

Complete God confidence knows that He *will* come through for us. He owns all the resources in the world, and He has a million and one ways to answer our needs when we place our trust in Him. I would have been okay if the money hadn't come in and I missed the trip, but God wanted to do some work in my heart during the trip, so He made a way for me to participate.

Hopefully, you know I'm not suggesting that God is a Santa Claus to whom we can casually give a list with all our whims, desires, and wants. Nor is He a magic genie who is ready to do whatever we want Him to do. But He *is* committed to meeting our needs and will sometimes use our waiting period as an opportunity to cause our faith to grow.

Having complete God confidence changes us! Because I'm from a Christian family with two parents who demonstrated God confidence themselves, I began to want what I saw in their lives. My family went to church regularly and was very involved. My closest friendships were from church. I grew up hearing the older folks testify about what God was doing in their lives, and as I listened and watched, I wanted the same God confidence I saw demonstrated around me.

So when I was nine years old, I asked Christ to come into my life and forgive my sins. I learned to place my confidence in Him while I was still in elementary school. And it changed my life. Later, when I was in high school, I knew I could boldly ask my heavenly Father for the money I needed for the mission trip, because my confidence in Him had already been established.

And at each stage in my life, that confidence in Him has grown, blossomed, and exploded. Through going to college, finding my first career job, and buying my first house, all the major points in my life have been saturated with confidence in Him. And because of that, He has helped me make wise decisions.

When I lived in Colorado, I had an opportunity to purchase a model home. I'd never had a new home before and was excited about the possibility. I prayed about the matter and made a long list. I told God that if everything on the list was answered, I'd know it was His will I purchase the house. One of the many things on the list was that I would be able to keep the new beautiful stainless steel refrigerator in the kitchen.

I gave my list to the Realtor and he laughed, but he told me he'd give it to the builder. He came back with the word that everything on my list had been approved *except* the fridge. That was close enough for me! After all, I was getting the other stuff—the furniture in the model home, the landscaping, and many more things. I wrote him a deposit check and went home.

God began to deal with me. *"Susie, I didn't answer your entire list, did I?"*

"Well, no. . .but only one thing was left on the list. I can easily buy a fridge."

"The deal was the entire list."

Because of my confidence in God, I knew He was right. I went back to the Realtor, told him I had jumped the gun, and got my check back. I explained my prayer to him and that God was certainly big enough to give me everything on my list.

The Realtor didn't understand. "Ma'am, I've never seen anyone get a list of demands as long as yours. What you've asked for and have been approved to get is huge!"

"I know, but it's not everything."

I was sad, because I really wanted the house. But I wanted to obey God more. Letting go of it felt like a death.

A few days later, the Realtor contacted me and said, "Your God must really be listening, because when I told the builder what you said, he agreed to give you the refrigerator. You have everything on your list."

I'm so glad I listened to God. And I'm grateful that confidence in Him makes a difference.

DAY 7

God Can Be Trusted

Then God said, "Take your son, your only son, whom you love—
Isaac—and go to the region of Moriah. Sacrifice him there
as a burnt offering on a mountain I will show you."
GENESIS 22:2

Abraham has been referred to as the "father of faith." He definitely demonstrated that faith when he said he'd follow God without knowing where he was going. Think about the confidence in God that move required! Wouldn't it be hard for you to sell your home, pack your belongings, and say to your family, "We're moving"?

"We are? Where?"

You clear your throat and respond, "Uh. . .I don't know."

"Wait a second! I'm in the school play. I can't just leave."

"And what about prom?"

"Your job. What will your boss say?"

"I don't fully understand it. I just know God is telling us to move."

"Okay. God is telling us to move is one thing. But I say waiting until we have all the details is the smart thing to do. We can't just *move* to where we don't know we're going!"

"No. I'm certain. God has told us to move. He's telling us to go *now*. And He will let us know one day at a time where we'll stay each night."

That's a lot of God confidence, isn't it? And there's so much more to the story that makes it even more fascinating! Abraham and his wife, Sarah, had been praying and yearning to have children. God told Abraham that He would give him a son and his descendants would eventually outnumber the stars in the sky. So when Sarah got pregnant at ninety years of age, Abraham, at one hundred, knew God was into miracles.

Abraham named his son Isaac, and he was cherished. A few years later, however, God gave Abraham an interesting command. According to today's scripture, He told Abraham to offer Isaac as an offering to the Lord. This means Abraham would have to bind and tie his son on an altar and kill him. *What?*

Father and son made their journey early the next morning. Abraham had learned that sheer obedience is what God desires. He was willing to obey. But he also had tremendous faith and knew that God loved him. Yes, surely, he was afraid as he walked with his son to the top of Mount Moriah. Yet his confidence in God was greater than his fear.

Abraham knew that God would never break His word, and God had promised that Isaac's descendants would someday outnumber the stars. So obviously, Isaac would need to live for that promise to come true. As Abraham raised his knife to his son on the altar, God's voice rang clear: "Stop, Abraham! I have provided a ram for your sacrifice." Abraham and Isaac quickly grabbed the loose ram and offered it to God.

This moment proved to be a significant turning point in Abraham's life. He would face other major decisions in the years to come, but when he did, his God confidence soared because of this unforgettable event.

How could Abraham have such complete God confidence when it came to his son—Abraham's dream come true?

Abraham knew something about God that we'd do well to remember: God never contradicts Himself. The God who said, "Thou shalt not kill," in the Ten Commandments (Exodus 20:13 KJV) wouldn't suddenly change His mind and make it okay to kill. Abraham knew God wouldn't contradict Himself. We, too, need to remember that God never goes against Himself or His word.

(You may be thinking, *But all through the Old Testament, God told His people time and time again to kill. Wouldn't that be a contradiction?* Different words are used for "murder" and "kill." The Greek is more specific, and because the Greek New Testament quotes the Hebrew Old Testament, Exodus 20:13 is best translated, "You shall not murder." Murder is the unlawful taking of life. Killing is the lawful taking of life. God says killing in self-defense is justifiable [see Exodus 22:2]. If mere killing of any kind were the issue, then God wouldn't say that killing in self-defense is permissible. This is the reason that modern translations say, "You shall not murder," instead of "You shall not kill.")

Abraham believed with all his heart that he could obey God because God would provide another sacrifice in His perfect timing. He knew if he would obey, God would honor His promise to give him offspring that would outnumber the stars—and that couldn't happen if Isaac were dead. Abraham acted in faith.

When the situation looks hopeless. . .when death seems imminent. . .when you don't understand the events in your life. . .you can have confidence in Jehovah God to keep His promises. This is the ideal. But what if you *don't* have God confidence? We'll look at Abraham's wife to see an example. (See Days 12 and 13.)

DAY 8

When Will You Move, God?

The LORD does not let the righteous go hungry,
but he thwarts the craving of the wicked.
PROVERBS 10:3

Chris was on staff in a two-hundred-member church and loved his role as visitation, discipleship, and prayer pastor. The older people especially loved him because he served with such tenderness. It was easy to sense his love and genuine concern with every conversation. He made several hospital calls each day, but he also spent quite a bit of time in the office to meet with people who stopped by the church for counsel or prayer.

Chris also enjoyed the times his senior pastor asked him to preach during his absence. The senior pastor had served a couple of decades at this specific church and was well into his eighties now. He had actually come to this church after retirement and begun serving as pastor again.

Like all churches, this one had its share of problems—people vying for control, some wanting the senior pastor to move on and a younger one to replace him, and so on.

Chris is a peacemaker and tried his best to calm those who created conflict, but trouble multiplied quickly. The pastor resigned and conflict increased. A new pastor arrived, and Chris assumed things would get better, but the new minister felt led to take the church in a different direction, and the situation only became more intolerable. Chris resigned.

"While all this was happening at the church, my grandmother [living in another state] was close to death, and my parents were also in poor health. So after much prayer, I heard God telling me to go home—where my parents and grandmother lived—several states away," he says.

Chris had been a Christian for several years and had complete God confidence. It would take quite a bit of his personal savings to move himself across the nation, and though he had no job once he arrived, he knew he was in the center of God's will.

He found a small one-bedroom apartment and immediately began applying for ministry positions while helping care for his parents and grandmother. He had a great résumé with wonderful experience but couldn't land a ministry job. With money running low, he began applying for secular jobs. "I just needed something to make rent until I could find a ministry job, so I was willing to take anything," he says.

Though he was *willing* to do anything, employers felt he was too talented for many of the jobs he was applying for, so he wasn't even able to get a job at burger joints. Months passed, and Chris had used almost all of his savings.

"I knew God had brought me here, but I really needed Him to affirm I was in the center of His will. Sometimes His voice is so clear it's almost audible. And other times He's silent, and I have to just trust His faithfulness. He was being silent, but my faith in Him was not wavering."

Chris loved clinging to a specific scripture: " 'For I know the plans I have for you,' declares the LORD, 'plans to prosper you and not to harm you, plans to give you hope and a future' " (Jeremiah 29:11).

"Every now and then," Chris says, "I'd receive a small check from someone in my former church or from a friend. So I knew God was taking care of me. I always had something to eat. I still had a roof over my head, but money was truly running out!"

Chris needed rent money and also had to make his car payment—along with insurance—so he began selling his furniture. He sold his TV, couch, and dining room table and was finally down to the bare essentials, but he still didn't have a job. "I continued to apply to every place available," he says. "I couldn't believe I wasn't getting *anything*. I mean you just assume you can always get a job flipping burgers!"

After eight months without a job, Chris had done all he could do. "At the end of another month, I knew I'd be living in my car," he says. "I had no more money for rent; I'd sold everything I could; I had applied for every possible job I could find—yet I still didn't have a job."

While many may have begun to doubt, Chris kept the faith. "It would have been very easy to start rethinking everything," he says. "Did God really tell me to resign the church? Had He really guided me back home? If so, why was I about to be homeless? I couldn't let myself go there. Instead, I focused on His faithfulness through the years. He had never failed me. He had provided for me after a divorce left me with a son to care for. He enabled me to provide a good home and life for my son [who's now married]. He had given me godly friends throughout the years. He had proven Himself faithful over and over again. So I continued to cling to His faithfulness."

Nine months after Chris had moved across the nation to help care for his folks and grandmother, a church thirty minutes away offered him the position of senior pastor. "Talk about perfect timing! I didn't have the money to stay one more day in my apartment. This church has a parsonage that I now live in—and they just did some amazing remodeling to it! So I'm out of apartment life with an actual home, and I'm in a church filled with people who love me and are excited about growing in Christ. God has never failed me. Life isn't always easy, but He never let me go hungry, and He has always met my needs. God confidence has definitely changed me for the better!"

DAY 9
God Made a Way

In all thy ways acknowledge him, and he shall direct thy paths.
PROVERBS 3:6 KJV

After thirteen years of being a stay-at-home mom, Amy reentered the work world. Though her dream was to become a nurse, she wanted to be a mom even more, and she loved the time spent at home with her children during their formative years.

"I loved everything about being a stay-at-home mom," Amy says. "I enjoyed walking them to school, having lunch with them, and simply *being* with them."

When her youngest child was five, Amy began taking night classes for a nursing degree. She had to complete several prerequisite classes before she could even apply for the nursing program at the local community college. "Going back to school in the evenings wasn't a big deal," she says. "It gave me a little break from my household routine while allowing me to enjoy pursuing my other passion—nursing."

Looking back, Amy sees God in every bit of the process. "He put all the right people in my life at just the right time for everything to fall perfectly in place. He brought a woman into my life whose son happened to play baseball with my middle son. We spent a lot of time at the baseball field watching our boys play. It was during a summer championship playoff that we began talking about my going back to school for nursing. She encouraged me in this goal."

It was also during this time that Amy and her husband needed insurance for their growing family. Her husband's job simply didn't provide the insurance that met their needs.

Amy mentioned to Maureen—her ballpark friend—that she was looking for a job. She didn't know it, but Maureen was one of the managers in the Emergency Department at the local hospital. She told Amy about an opening for a job that she could easily do while continuing her nursing degree and get some firsthand experience with helping patients.

"I was hired, and my role was emergency support staff— sort of like a nursing assistant—CNA/PCA. I worked during the day and continued to complete my prerequisites at night so I could eventually apply to the nursing program."

Fast-forward two years and Amy found herself entering the nursing program. It was during this time that she had to change her work schedule from weekdays to weekends. "The program was only offered on weekdays, and there weren't any night classes," she remembers.

"My boys were very active in baseball at this time and were even on traveling teams. Many people in town remember me bringing my books to the ball fields to study while the games were being played. So going to the weekend work shift meant

I'd miss all the ball games, but even more importantly, I'd miss attending church with my family."

On her way to work the first weekend, Amy began to cry. "I prayed and asked God if I was truly doing the right thing," she says. "I just hated the fact that I'd be missing church. Every time the doors were open, we were there. This was something that had begun in my childhood and was now important to me as an adult. I wanted our children to realize the value of being consistent in our church attendance. I desired for them to know that church doesn't revolve around us—we make our schedules revolve around church. It's that important."

Amy's tears and prayers continued on her way to work, and by the time she pulled into the parking lot, God had given her that overwhelming peace that comes only from Him. "He reminded me that this was only temporary and that He had it all under control," she says.

"I knew He had provided the job, the hours, and the acceptance into the program. He was with me the entire time. I was confident in knowing that the path I was taking was exactly where He wanted me to be."

Fast-forward another two years and Amy found herself with the degree for which she'd worked so hard. She passed the state boards for her registered nurse's license and was immediately hired for a weekday position within the same department. She's a clinical supervisor in the Emergency

Department and loves what she does.

"I serve a God who is so totally in control of details that He provided a job that got me off weekends the very week after graduation! None of this would have been possible without Him," she says. "Through the entire process, He consistently increased my confidence in Him."

DAY 10

Change That Lasts a Lifetime

Then I heard the voice of the Lord saying, "Whom shall I send? And who will go for us?" And I said, "Here am I. Send me!"
ISAIAH 6:8

"When I was fourteen years old, I participated in a mission trip to Lima, Peru," Cara says. "I love horses and had made friends with the guy who kept the horses at El Pueblo—the place our group of four hundred was staying. I say we were friends, but that's kind of a stretch. I communicated with him through gestures, smiles, and my limited knowledge of Spanish—his native language."

This worker's name was Jesus (pronounced *Hay-soos*). He seemed interested in the group and in what they were doing. The more Cara prayed for him, the clearer she felt that God wanted her to give him a Spanish Bible.

"But I literally argued with God for several days," she says. "It was one thing to go out on the streets and talk about Christ with crowds of strangers. It would be quite another thing to give a Bible to someone with whom I was making a connection. Wouldn't he think I was weird? Or even worse—that I was flirting with him by giving him a gift?"

Cara had given away all of her Spanish Bibles, but she couldn't ignore God's prompting any longer. "I eventually gave in to this crazy urge and got a Spanish New Testament from one of my roommates. I took the Bible in a plastic bag with me when I went to ride the horses—as I usually did during free time—and I gave it to him.

"I'll never forget the look on his face as he opened it," she remembers. "He gingerly asked if it was really for him. I will forever remember riding the smooth-gaited Peruvian Paso horse as Jesus jogged off to the side, his eyes cemented onto the Bible he was paging through."

Cara's confidence in God soared. She had done the right thing, and it felt so good to be obedient to the nudging of the Holy Spirit within her. "I don't know what came of it," she says. "I only saw Jesus a few times after that. Our group left at the end of the week. I hope to see him again this side of heaven, though I know the possibility is rather remote. But through that act of obedience, God has continued to strengthen my confidence in Him. I've learned that when He guides me to do something, He will give me the strength to obey."

These days God is still using Cara overseas, but He seems to have turned her heart to the Middle East. Last year she taught English in Turkey and had a vast number of God moments there as well. Today? Cara is studying for final exams in her Introductory Turkish class at Indiana University and meeting Turkish people left and right.

"I often fail," Cara says, "but God just keeps loving me

anyway, and because *He* never fails, my confidence in Him keeps soaring!"

Cara is learning to follow God's will and to live in the center of His will. Sometimes, though, Christians struggle with knowing what God's will is. When we doubt His will, it affects our confidence in Him. When we're sure of His will, it increases our God confidence. So let's chat briefly about how to know God's will.

God often reveals His will to us through our desires: "Take delight in the LORD, and he will give you your heart's desires" (Psalm 37:4 NLT). *Cool. I desire a BMW,* you may be tempted to think. God isn't a magic genie, but He *does* place desires in our hearts to guide us into His will. Chances are that God isn't going to direct you to do something you hate.

He *will* guide you according to the gifts He has given you. For example, I'm terrible at math. I don't understand it, I don't like it, and it completely unnerves me. I know God isn't going to call me into accounting. That's not where I'm gifted, nor is it where my desires are.

Because He has gifted me with communication skills, He *does* expect me to use those gifts to communicate Him through speaking and writing. And when I do that, the desires of my heart are met.

Using the gifts He gives us = receiving the desires of our heart = growing confidence in God. These three things fit together perfectly and actually enhance each other.

CONSEQUENCES OF NOT HAVING GOD CONFIDENCE

DAY 11
Failure to Mature

Dear brothers, I have been talking to you as though you were still just babies in the Christian life who are not following the Lord but your own desires; I cannot talk to you as I would to healthy Christians who are filled with the Spirit. I have had to feed you with milk and not with solid food because you couldn't digest anything stronger. And even now you still have to be fed on milk. For you are still only baby Christians, controlled by your own desires, not God's.
1 CORINTHIANS 3:1–3 TLB

During the apostle Paul's first visit to the Christians in Corinth, he was disappointed that they weren't growing in their faith. They were still spiritual babies. Their spiritual muscles weren't developed; they couldn't digest "meat"—or the deeper things of Christ. Instead, they were still crawling in their faith.

Hebrews 6:1 gives Christians extreme clarity about spiritual growth: "Let us stop going over the same old ground again and again, always teaching those first lessons about Christ. Let us go on instead to other things and become mature in our understanding, as strong Christians ought to be" (TLB). The Corinthian Christians were still in spiritual kindergarten—only digesting the very basic truths and not going past that.

When we celebrate a new physical birth, our attention is on the baby. We take photos and movies and exclaim all over social media how cute he is. As a baby grows, however, we're not consumed with taking photos every day of his life. If we were, the child would become used to all the attention—and even learn to expect it. He would become a spoiled, self-willed child.

Unfortunately, some Christians fall into this category. When Johnny first gave his life to Christ, all eyes were on him. People were excited that he'd made a commitment to follow God. The attention felt good. But unless Johnny grows in his faith and moves away from self-centeredness, he'll become easily upset when he doesn't get his way, when others don't have time for him, or when he's left out.

Unfortunately, many church boards have baby Johnny Christians sitting around their conference tables. When a baby Christian feels strongly that the church carpet should be blue instead of beige, and no one else agrees with him, he's the one who turns it into a big deal instead of quietly dismissing the subject.

Physical babies need to be cuddled. Spiritual babies need to be handled with kid gloves. Physical babies cry when they can't have what they want when they want it. Spiritual babies cause friction and hold grudges when people around them don't cave in to their whims and ideas. Babies are great at receiving, but they don't know how to give.

It's easy to see why the apostle Paul was discouraged when he visited Corinth, isn't it? He fully expected to find mature Christians—people excited about giving, sharing their faith, and living out the deeper truths of scripture. Instead, he found baby Christians arguing, demanding their own way, and refusing to grow spiritually.

Let's say that Craig refused to leave kindergarten. When he turned six, he talked his parents into letting him repeat the year. What if he kept doing this year after year? Can you imagine a twenty-one-year-old still in kindergarten? "Well, I was afraid to move on," Craig says. "I didn't want to have to write essays, and I loved taking a nap after recess, and I didn't want to learn story problems because I was afraid I'd fail. So I decided to stay in kindergarten where it doesn't matter if I color outside the lines or ever learn to read books without pictures."[1]

As silly as that is, many Christians refuse to graduate from "spiritual kindergarten." And that's why they never develop complete God confidence.

It's God's will, however, that we mature in our faith. If we refuse to "grow up" spiritually, we limit God's working in and through our lives. For example, no one can argue the mighty way He has ministered through the Reverend Billy Graham through the years. If, however, Reverend Graham hadn't bothered reading and studying the Bible and hadn't spent time in prayer to grow his faith, God wouldn't have been able to use him to make the impact he has.

Churches are filled with "sleeping Christians"—folks who talk about God, smile, and act kindly toward one another but who rarely grow stronger in their faith.

LifeWay Research surveyed more than 2,900 Protestant churchgoers and found that while 90 percent "desire to please and honor Jesus in all I do," only 19 percent personally read the Bible every day.[2]

"Sleeping Christians" are baby Christians. They don't have much God confidence. And while they wonder why their faith in God isn't stronger, the dust on their Bibles shouts the reason. Let's grow up!

1. Check out "Faith in Kindergarten"—a video by Bluefish on YouTube—to see this scenario acted out: https://www.youtube.com/watch?v=51gV7Buufx8.
2. Jeremy Weber, "80% of Churchgoers Don't Read Bible Daily, LifeWay Survey Suggests," *ChristianityToday.com*, September 27, 2012, http://www.christianitytoday.com/gleanings/2012/september/80-of-churchgoers-dont-read-bible-daily-lifeway-survey.html.

DAY 12

Lacking God Confidence

Now Sarai, Abram's wife, had borne him no children. But she had an Egyptian slave named Hagar; so she said to Abram, "The LORD has kept me from having children. Go, sleep with my slave; perhaps I can build a family through her." Abram agreed to what Sarai said. So after Abram had been living in Canaan ten years, Sarai his wife took her Egyptian slave Hagar and gave her to her husband to be his wife. He slept with Hagar, and she conceived.
GENESIS 16:1–4

(If you need a reminder of Abraham and Sarah's story, flip back to Day 7.)

Let's rewind a few steps to the time *before* Sarah had given birth to Isaac.

Sarah (God later changed Sarai's name to Sarah and Abram's name to Abraham) was aware of God's promise to bless her and Abraham with descendants who would outnumber the stars. But after living in Canaan for ten years and still not conceiving, Sarah became impatient.

Oftentimes when God says He's going to do something, we expect that He means *now*. But He's on a completely different timetable than we are. We'd be wise to react like David did when he was told he would be king of Israel. He didn't toss his shepherd's staff in the dust and rush out to purchase a new wardrobe and search for an empty throne.

He simply continued caring for his flock of sheep. His confidence in God was so strong that he knew God would work out all the details when it was time. Years passed, and David consistently performed his duties as a shepherd.

King Saul received word that David would eventually take his place on the throne, and he made plans to kill David. But David's confidence in God remained strong. He left his home, fled into the mountains, and hid in caves, but His confidence in God never wavered.

David probably wondered when God's promise would come true. When would he actually get to be king? But he refused to take things into his own hands and make it happen. He waited patiently on God to move in God's perfect timing.

If we could learn this lesson, it would remove a lot of pressure from us, wouldn't it? We wouldn't worry about how or when the details would come together; we'd simply know that we could wait in peace until God moved.

We live in a fast-paced culture. We want everything *now*. We zoom up to the drive-through, toss our money through the window, and catch our food as we hit the gas. It's no wonder we live spiritually the same way. Toss a prayer request into the toaster and expect the answer to pop right out. Sometimes God's ways take time.

God told Moses He would lead the Israelites to a specific portion of land He had designated as the Promised Land, yet it took more than forty years for them to arrive. And though the Israelites often disobeyed Moses, threatened him, and rebelled against him, Moses kept his confidence in God. He knew the secret of waiting on God's perfect timing. He had seen God's faithfulness in the past, and he knew he could trust God to keep His word in the future. Instead of rushing God, Moses consistently followed.

Unfortunately, we often try to be microwave Christians. What if God is calling us to be slow cooker Christians? Maybe He wants us to cook in His grace a bit longer. Perhaps He desires for us to enjoy the savor of His Spirit in us and through us. Maybe He simply wants us to wait on Him.

Sarah hadn't learned this lesson. She didn't have the God confidence she needed. Sarah began to doubt, and instead of waiting on God's perfect timing, she decided to take things into her own hands. She commanded her Egyptian servant, Hagar, to sleep with Abraham so he could begin the line of descendants God had promised him.

Hagar became pregnant from Abraham and gave birth to a boy she named Ishmael. Abraham was eighty-six years old when Ishmael was born. Sarah, meanwhile, was still childless. By taking things into her own hands and not waiting on God's perfect plan, she really messed things up.

Why didn't she wait on God? She didn't have faith. Having God confidence changes everything. Not having it also changes everything—but always for the worse.

DAY 13
Still No Confidence

When she knew she was pregnant, she began to despise her mistress. Then Sarai said to Abram, "You are responsible for the wrong I am suffering. I put my slave in your arms, and now that she knows she is pregnant, she despises me. May the LORD judge between you and me." "Your slave is in your hands," Abram said. "Do with her whatever you think best." Then Sarai mistreated Hagar; so she fled from her.
GENESIS 16:4–6

Sarah probably didn't wait on God for some of the same reasons we don't:

- We become impatient.
- We begin to doubt that we heard God correctly.
- We think we can work it out better and faster than He will.
- When we don't see Him working, we become afraid and we let fear move us to action instead of being still.
- When we don't see Him move, we assume He's not moving.

When Sarah was much older, she experienced the fulfillment of God's promise through the birth of her own son, Isaac. And unfortunately, here's where the story takes an interesting turn: As Isaac and Ishmael began to grow, Sarah became jealous of Hagar and her son. Yes, even though it was Sarah's idea to use Hagar to give Abraham a son, now that Isaac was on the scene, Sarah wanted nothing to do with Ishmael.

She burned with anger when she saw her husband teaching Ishmael to fish and when she saw Isaac, Abraham, and Ishmael hunting together, wrestling, or playfully teaching one another. Sarah knew that both boys would eventually share Abraham's inheritance, and she unfairly wanted it all for her own son, Isaac.

When we step ahead of God, we mess things up. Yes, He can still make beautiful things from our mistakes, but how much better if we simply trust Him and wait on His perfect plan! When we don't see God moving, it doesn't mean He's not working on our behalf. He's always moving; most of the time He's working quietly behind the scenes.

Sarah demonstrated her lack of God confidence in usurping His position of authority in her life and taking charge. And what does this tell us? It shows that her relationship with God wasn't as strong as it could have been. Who held the prominent place in her life? Not Jehovah. It was Abraham, and later it became Isaac.

For us to become all God desires us to be, He has to have complete authority in our lives. He wants our love and devotion directed to Him first and to our spouse and family next. When we place God above all else, our faith in Him grows and He blesses our faith.

Though Ishmael (born of Hagar) and Isaac (born of Sarah) were both Abraham's sons, there were many differences between the two boys. Ishmael's birth was of the flesh. It wasn't different from any other birth between a man and a woman. Isaac's birth, however, was brought about by God's promise. Sarah was ninety-one when Isaac was born. She was long past her years of bearing a child. Physically, it was impossible. But God keeps His promises. And He touched Sarah's physical body, enabling her to receive Abraham's seed and give birth to Isaac. Sure, it was a physical birth—but it was also a spiritual birth. God had made the impossible possible.

We find here a bit of foreshadowing of God's plan for humanity through His Son, Jesus. Though He had not yet sent Jesus into the world, we can see the foreshadowing here of a spiritual birth for us—that God makes the impossible possible. We can't enter heaven with sin, and we are sinful creatures. Yet because God sent His only Son, Jesus Christ, we can experience a spiritual birth and become new children in His name.

Abraham and Sarah tried to hurry God's promise along through Hagar, but we learn that God doesn't need help in fulfilling His promises. Instead, He desires our faith, our obedience, and our complete willingness to trust His ways even though they may seem slow.

Because of Sarah's lack of God confidence, the two boys—Isaac and Ishmael—eventually became two rival nations that are still at war today.

Another who lacked God confidence? Judas—the disciple who betrayed Christ. Many Bible scholars believe that Judas was tired of hearing about Christ's kingdom that would be set in place *someday*. Judas wanted action now. He was a member of a political group known as the Zealots, and many Bible scholars believe that Judas never meant for Christ to be killed; he simply wanted to "hurry along" the plan of setting up the kingdom.

Judas failed to realize that Christ's kingdom would not be a kingdom that would blast the Romans and set itself up on earth in Judas's time. Christ spoke of an eternal kingdom—a kingdom of peace and joy and perfection in God.

But by betraying Jesus to the religious authorities, Judas thought it would force Jesus to declare Himself as King and quickly establish His kingdom. Instead, Jesus allowed Himself to be crucified to forgive our sins so that we may enter His kingdom with Him. When Judas realized Jesus was not going to do things the way he expected, he hanged himself.

Like Sarah, Judas lacked faith. He couldn't wait on God's perfect timing. When we try to take God's plans into our own hands, we always have to face the consequences. Have faith.

DAY 14

Disobedience Costs

*When the woman saw that the fruit of the tree was good
for food and pleasing to the eye, and also desirable for
gaining wisdom, she took some and ate it. She also gave
some to her husband, who was with her, and he ate it.*
GENESIS 3:6

When you hear the word *paradise*, what comes to your mind?
Do you see images of Maui, Tahiti, the Maldives, St. Barts,
Nantucket Island, or other beaches you've visited or read
about? God created a paradise that outdid any image we can
imagine. The Garden of Eden was perfection. It was lush,
green, and filled with a variety of fruit trees offering ripe,
juicy favorites. Soft green grass lined the grounds, and tame
animals of every species gently ambled between the trees and
over the hills.

This is where Adam and Eve were created. God gently
scooped a handful of dirt in His hands, and as He rubbed it
between His fingers, He brought forth man and named him
Adam. By giving Adam the gift of this perfect paradise and
everything in it, He was actually handing him the deed to
planet Earth.

After giving Adam life, God removed a rib from Adam
and formed Eve from it. The two enjoyed the beautiful

paradise of Eden. This was their world, and they had all they wanted. God had only one rule: Don't eat of the fruit from the tree in the center of the garden.

The two humans and their Creator enjoyed intimate fellowship and complete fulfillment in the garden.

For a while.

Then Satan, who is known as the "father of lies," entered the scene and began tempting Eve to eat the forbidden fruit. Adam and Eve were pure, innocent, good. They had enjoyed living in complete obedience to God.

But when Eve ate the forbidden fruit, she was immediately exposed to sin. When she shared the fruit with Adam, he, too, suddenly knew sin. With sin in their lives, they quickly transitioned from an innocent, naive couple to disobedient people who now saw things as Satan saw them. They realized they were naked. They now knew what fear was and ran from God. Don't you want to push the PAUSE button and jump inside the story and plead with Eve?

"You have a perfect life, Eve! Don't mess it up by disobeying God. You don't know pain, sickness, confusion, or rejection. These negatives will become part of your life if you disobey."

Can you imagine living in a perfect world such as Eden? The rosebushes had no thorns. The ground didn't have to be tilled. There was no such thing as jealousy, revenge, or anger. Life was composed of peace, laughter, harmony, and contentment.

Scripture tells us that Adam's and Eve's eyes were opened and they noticed they were naked. Again, don't you want to jump inside the story and say, "Hey! Who told you that you were naked?" They covered themselves with fig leaves because they were embarrassed. Their childlike innocence was now gone. This knowledge of nakedness would lead to feelings of insecurity, comparison, lust, and envy.

What could have been!

Their lives had started perfectly. Adam and Eve were filled with God confidence. What happened? They let down their guard. They took their eyes off God. They listened to the wrong voice. Disobedience always costs! They were cast out of the perfect garden, and the entire world changed with sin.

The animals became wild, the earth experienced storms, the ground became entangled with thorns, Adam and Eve experienced pain—*all* of creation was affected and groaned. And the deed to planet Earth was now in Satan's hands. Hope was not lost, though!

God restored Adam's and Eve's faith, but their disobedience affected everyone and everything. Their son Cain killed his brother Abel. Jealousy, anger, and evil exploded into wars, epidemics, and rape.

But someday the deed to planet Earth will be back in the right hands. From this very first book of the Bible (Genesis), we see the deed transferred from God to Adam to Satan. In the very last book of the Bible (Revelation), we see it transferred from Satan to God to Jesus Christ.

The apostle John was the last of the twelve disciples to die. Before his death, he was exiled to the island of Patmos. While there, he received the Revelation of Jesus Christ. In Revelation 4 we see that John has received a backstage pass to heaven and is seeing things inside heaven and on the earth that no one else has seen. In chapter 5 we see him weeping because no one is worthy to open the seven-sealed scroll, the deed to planet Earth. An angel approaches John and comforts him. "You don't need to weep, John. There is One who is worthy to open the scroll. His name is Jesus Christ."

Christ opens the scroll, and the great tribulation—the end times—begins. By opening the scroll, He is proclaiming that He is taking control back from Satan and the deed is once again in the hands of the Creator. This should give every Christian ultimate God confidence!

DAY 15

You Can Run, but You Can't Hide

But Jonah ran away from the LORD and headed for Tarshish.
He went down to Joppa, where he found a ship bound for
that port. After paying the fare, he went aboard and
sailed for Tarshish to flee from the LORD.
JONAH 1:3

Because Jonah was a prophet, he was accustomed to being sent to a variety of places by God to share His truth. This was his appointed "job" from God Himself. But when the Lord instructed him to go to Nineveh, Jonah rebelled. He knew all about Nineveh. Sure, they needed God's salvation. They absolutely needed to repent and give their lives to a God who would forgive and love and lead them to live holy lives.

But Jonah knew the reputation of the Ninevites. He knew they were cruel people. In fact, another prophet—Nahum—called Nineveh the "bloody city." Not only were they extremely cruel, but they boasted about their acts of cruelty on monuments that exist in museums today. Enduring Word Media lists a few of the boasts that are inscribed on monuments:

"I cut off their heads and formed them into pillars."
"Bubo, son of Buba, I flayed in the city of Arbela and I

> *spread his skin upon the city wall."*
>
> *"I flayed all the chief men who had revolted, and I covered the pillar with their skins."*
>
> *"I cut off the limbs of the. . .royal officers who had rebelled."*
>
> *"3,000 captives I burned with fire."*
>
> *"I cut off their noses, their ears, and their fingers, of many I put out their eyes."*[1]

The Ninevites used human skin in making furniture. Naturally, Jonah was frightened by what he'd heard. These people often forced parents to watch their children being burned alive just before the parents themselves were murdered.

Entire cities had been known to commit suicide rather than fall into the hands of the Ninevites. Jonah was also disgusted with their sin. He knew they worshipped idols. The Ninevites weren't Jewish, and Jonah could have been a racist. Furthermore, it was common knowledge that the Assyrians (Ninevites) were planning to destroy the people of God (Israelites).

So when Jonah heard that God wanted him to evangelize Nineveh, he headed two thousand miles in the opposite direction. This was as far as he could travel to get away from God. Jonah was thinking he could outsmart God. But when we read Psalm 139:7–10, we discover that God always knows where we are! This passage tells us we can *never* hide from God.

But Jonah was determined to try! So he boarded a ship headed for Tarshish located on the western coast of Spain. Where was his God confidence? Why didn't he know that if God asked him to do something, God would protect him, strengthen him, and enable him to do the job?

From the beginning, it seemed as though Jonah had a chip on his shoulder. Perhaps he was simply a difficult person to get along with. We all know someone like that— one who's never really happy. Jonah probably always had something to complain about. He was still being used of God, but he was a reluctant prophet who was harboring a critical spirit within. The bottom line: Jonah didn't want the Ninevites to be forgiven! He was angry with them and wanted to see them pay for their sins.

God is gracious and forgiving. Unfortunately, His prophet Jonah wasn't. So off he went. . .to get away from God. When we run from God, Satan will always tempt us with what seems to be an easy way out. And sure enough, there was a ship just about to pull away. Jonah purchased a ticket, climbed aboard, and thought he'd outwitted God.

But God is always one step ahead of us! He sent a terrible storm. Jonah was thrown overboard and was swallowed by a giant fish. Imagine the stabbing pain he must have felt as he brushed across the teeth and how hard it would have been to breathe as he slid down a slimy esophagus to the stomach.

The odor itself probably knocked him unconscious. And the heat would have been unbearable. Swimming inside of gastric juices and with other swallowed fish and debris, Jonah certainly had time to think. . .and to pray. After he repented and told God he was ready to obey, the fish vomited Jonah right where God wanted him—on the shores of Nineveh.

There's a good chance that the acid inside the fish bleached Jonah to an albino white. He also may have lost his hair. At any rate, he was quite the spectacle standing in the middle of the city square. His presence demanded attention.

When he spoke, people listened. And reacted. In fact, the king's heart was repentant, and he ordered all the people to confess their sins and get right with God.

Wow! What an ending. It was a great ending for Nineveh, but it wasn't such a great ending for Jonah. Instead of rejoicing in the salvation of a nation, he complained to God. "This is what I knew would happen. I knew You'd forgive them if they repented." Jonah still had a bad attitude.

We don't know what happened to this reluctant prophet. But we can surmise that unless he sought forgiveness for his critical attitude and established God confidence, he never became all that God desired of him.

The story could have ended with a giant celebration: the prophet Jonah and the entire nation celebrating God's goodness and His forgiveness of sins. But because of Jonah's lack of God confidence, the ending is bittersweet.

1. David Guzik, "Nahum 3—Nineveh, the Wicked City," EnduringWord. com, 2001, www.enduringword.com/commentaries/3403.htm.

GOD CONFIDENCE HELPS US IN DIFFICULT RELATIONSHIPS

DAY 16
God Dreams Bigger

Now glory be to God, who by his mighty power at work within us is able to do far more than we would ever dare to ask or even dream of—infinitely beyond our highest prayers, desires, thoughts, or hopes.
EPHESIANS 3:20 TLB

Conner had been dating her boyfriend for almost two years. Without any warning, he declared he wanted to date another girl, and the relationship ended. "We both claimed to be Christians," she says, "but neither one of us was chasing after Jesus as we should have been. I was blinded by love.

"Though I was definitely hurt and confused. . .I was also amazed by my confidence in God. Although my heart was breaking, God kept reminding me that I was beautiful, cherished, and loved by Him—the King of the world! I knew I could be confident in His unfailing promises because He is faithful."

Conner was still confused, though. She wondered how God could allow her heart to hurt so badly. She was frustrated and angry. "I noticed, however, that as I began seeking God instead of questioning Him, my heart began to change. My goal became to know the heart of God. And that pursuit changed everything!"

Conner soon realized that because God loves her so

much, He wants to protect her. "I no longer felt angry at God. Instead, I found myself slowly becoming grateful for protecting me from something that would have eventually destroyed me," she says.

"It was hard for me to imagine that God could bring someone better into my life, because at that time I thought I had the best guy in the world." Before the breakup, the plan was to graduate from college, get married, and Conner would pursue a graduate degree in school psychology. "This had been my dream for the past few years," she remembers. "I felt the relationship and the dream ending together. So what would I do for a career? I felt so lost! And I'd already accepted a fall internship with a school psychologist."

Conner went ahead and began her internship but soon discovered school psychology wasn't where her heart was. "I hated it!" she says. "I couldn't imagine spending my life in that area. It just wasn't me." Conner spent her entire Christmas break seeking God's will about what she should do. What was His plan for her? Where should she go?

"My roommate was planning on attending seminary after she graduated, and she invited me to visit the campus with her. It was amazing," Conner says. "As I walked through the campus, everything felt so good—so right. I sensed God tugging on my heart and leading me to pursue a seminary degree. I'm now deeply involved in my studies at the seminary, and I'm loving it! I know this is exactly where I'm supposed to be. I'm not sure yet where God will place me after seminary graduation, but I trust Him."

Conner says she has definitely learned a lot from her breakup, but the biggest thing she has learned is that she is God's daughter. "I can walk confidently because the God of the universe is my Daddy. He loves me more than I can imagine. He doesn't always give me the answers I want immediately, but in His perfect timing He reveals His will to me. I'm currently not in a relationship, and I don't feel sad or inadequate because of it. Instead, I feel truly satisfied in Christ."

Is God calling Conner to remain single, or will He bring a man into her life? "If I am called to singleness, it's okay," she says. "Being single has allowed me to do many more things for God's kingdom than I could if I were involved in a dating relationship.

"Right now I'm not worried about a boyfriend or a husband. Sure, I wish there was someone bringing me flowers and telling me I'm pretty. But for right now, I know that Christ has chosen me and is pursuing my heart more than any man ever could."

We can have confidence in One who always dreams bigger for us than we dream for ourselves. By allowing our confidence in Him to grow, we learn to live in the very center of His will. And there's not a better feeling in the world than being in the center of God's will.

DAY 17

Friends Are Friends Forever?

After some time Paul said to Barnabas, "Let's go back and visit each city where we previously preached the word of the Lord, to see how the new believers are doing." Barnabas agreed and wanted to take along John Mark. But Paul disagreed strongly, since John Mark had deserted them in Pamphylia and had not continued with them in their work. Their disagreement was so sharp that they separated. Barnabas took John Mark with him and sailed for Cyprus.
ACTS 15:36–39 NLT

The apostles Paul and Barnabas had enjoyed an amazing friendship. You may recall that Paul was formerly known as Saul—the one who hunted Christians and killed them. But when God temporarily blinded him on the road to the city of Damascus (where Paul was planning to kill more Christians), he fell in the street and paid attention to what God had to say.

God revealed Himself to Saul, convicted him of his sins, demonstrated His love for him, and changed his name to Paul. That's quite a bit of action in a short amount of time! After God returned Paul's sight, word spread to the Christians that their enemy had become a believer. You can imagine, however, why it was hard for many of them to believe. They were uncertain because of Paul's reputation and still feared for their lives.

The name *Barnabas* means "one who encourages," and he was quick to live up to this definition. He was known as an encourager among the early Christians, and when Barnabas pleaded with the church to believe Paul and to have faith in his new relationship with God, the Christians took the word of Barnabas.

Though Barnabas hadn't personally known Paul, because of his own God confidence, he accepted the testimony of this new Christian brother. Together they helped the other apostles organize and develop many new churches and spread the Gospel of salvation.

But we read in today's scripture that they had a disagreement. Remember, both were godly men and were excited about sharing the Gospel and planting new churches. However, this disagreement regarding their next missionary journey wasn't a minor argument. It was full-blown opposition between them.

Paul and Barnabas had taken John Mark on a previous mission journey, and he wasn't able to make it to the end. Mark was a younger man (probably in his late teens) who frequently got sick and wasn't used to traveling away from home. Not only was he physically ill, but he was also homesick and missed his mother. Bible scholars believe she was a single mom, because Mark's father isn't mentioned. Paul probably viewed Mark as a "mama's boy" and was frustrated that he couldn't make the entire journey and quit halfway through. Barnabas, however, probably viewed Mark as a young man who was a great help to his mother and genuinely cared about her needs.

So when the encourager Barnabas wanted to give Mark a second chance and show that he believed in him, Paul wouldn't hear of it. "He blew the chance we gave him! Why give him another? The work we're doing isn't for the faint of heart. He can't cut it."

Again, both men had amazing God confidence. Both were serving God and desired to do what was right. But they reached a point in their relationship where they simply couldn't agree, and it cost them their friendship. Sometimes we mistakenly assume that just because people are Christians, they'll agree and love working with each other.

But because God has created each one of us with a unique personality and a different set of gifts and skills, this isn't always true.

We can be solid Christians yet disagree with a Christian brother or sister. The key? Do it in love, and don't let the disagreement affect your confidence in God.

Paul was certainly used in a mighty way by God. He wrote much of the New Testament and was instrumental in planting several churches. He even brought the Gospel to the Gentiles! Yet he was also stubborn sometimes and perhaps got in the way of the fruit of the Spirit shining through him. For example, in this case we certainly don't see patience or gentleness, do we?

We are all continuous works of God. Thankfully, God is not finished with us yet, and He wasn't finished with Paul. The disagreement between the two leaders was unsurpassable, so Paul finally went one way with Silas, and Barnabas and Mark went the other way. God used both teams.

Let's fast-forward. We see that years later Paul has matured spiritually and aged physically. As he writes to his young friend Timothy, he personally asks for Mark to join him. "Only Luke is with me. Get Mark and bring him with you, because he is helpful to me in my ministry" (2 Timothy 4:11).

Paul had seen Mark mature through the years, and now the elderly apostle realized God was using Mark in ministry. Apparently Mark had been able to encourage many of Paul's converts and even enhance some of the ministry Paul left behind. "He is helpful to me in my ministry." Paul was seeing Mark's ministry gifts and skills.

Three men who were full of God confidence continued in ministry in spite of misunderstandings. And we see the fruit of Mark's God confidence all through the Gospel of Mark. That's right—he is the author.

DAY 18
A Deadly Dance

On Herod's birthday the daughter of Herodias danced for the guests and pleased Herod so much that he promised with an oath to give her whatever she asked. Prompted by her mother, she said, "Give me here on a platter the head of John the Baptist." The king was distressed, but because of his oaths and his dinner guests, he ordered that her request be granted and had John beheaded in the prison.
MATTHEW 14:6–10

John the Baptist was a fascinating person. He was called the "forerunner of Christ." In other words, God had appointed him to pave the way for Jesus. John's job was to "set the stage"—to get people ready for Jesus' announcement of being the long-awaited Messiah.

John didn't mince words. He called sin what it was: sin. And in doing so, he often stepped on toes. John was a loner. He lived in the wilderness, and his clothing was made from animal skins. He didn't care about fashion, what people thought of him, or having a social life. He was simply focused on fulfilling his calling in life.

He smelled bad. He yelled at people. He ate bugs. And because he did what he was supposed to do—show people their sin—he didn't have many friends. One especially difficult relationship was with King Herod.

The ruler was sleeping with Herodias—his sister-in-law. John the Baptist told the king that he was living in sin and that God's wrath would be on him if he continued this kind of lifestyle. No one likes to have one's toes stepped on—especially an authority figure. John's message infuriated Herod, and he had the prophet thrown into prison.

Meanwhile the king continued to live in debauchery and decided to throw a lavish party. The banquet hall was packed. The food was exquisite. The wine flowed freely. The entertainment was. . .close to home. You see, Herod had hired the daughter of Herodias to perform a sensuous dance that was so provocative the guests had to drink more wine to feel less guilty about watching.

Herod was tantalized. He was so pleased with the pornography in motion that he loudly boasted he would give the girl anything she wanted—even up to half his kingdom. Never having been offered such a large paycheck, she quickly consulted with her mom for guidance.

Herodias didn't think twice. "Tell the king you want the head of John the Baptist," she whispered as a wicked smile spread across her lips. "On a platter."

When Herod heard what she wanted, his heart sank. Even though he was disgusted with John, he didn't want to kill him. He halfway enjoyed listening to him preach. But the announcement had already been made, and now that his guests had heard the odd request, he couldn't back down—not in front of this esteemed crowd.

So with a heavy heart, Herod ordered the beheading of John, and just as requested, his head was brought to the girl on a platter.

Let's recap where John was. He was in prison. And he was there for announcing that Herod was living in sin. John could have easily recanted. "Well, I didn't actually mean to call it *sin*, Your Majesty. It's just not a good idea. Let me help you create a ten-step plan to get out of this mess."

John didn't back down from the truth. How could he remain so strong in the face of his adversary—the one he knew would eventually kill him? He had God confidence. John knew that the same God who empowered him with strength to speak out in boldness would also empower him with strength to die without compromising.

John's goal wasn't to make friends. He wasn't focused on being a people pleaser. He was simply committed to God's call on his life. Thank God for pastors, missionaries, and evangelists who are committed to preaching God's truth no matter the cost. Oftentimes, following that call comes at a great price. Yet doesn't it cost *all* of us everything to follow God?

Luke 14:28 reminds us that it would be silly to build a house without knowing the cost. Likewise, Christ tells us to know the cost of following Him before we announce our plan publicly. He clearly lets us know that being His disciple is an all-or-nothing response. He calls us to follow Him, and we are to do so with 100 percent abandon. And as we do? Our God confidence multiplies!

When Elisha was called to be discipled (or mentored) by the prophet Elijah, he responded in a radical way. "So Elisha left him and went back. He took his yoke of oxen and slaughtered them. He burned the plowing equipment to cook the meat and gave it to the people, and they ate. Then he set out to follow Elijah and became his servant" (1 Kings 19:21).

Elisha didn't want to be tempted to quit and return home, so he destroyed his manner of living. His God confidence had taught him that his heavenly Father would provide all he needed.

Back to John the Baptist. Long before he was thrown into a dark, damp prison cell, John had settled the issue. He knew he would have difficult relationships because of his higher commitment to God. He was okay with being misunderstood and mistreated because of the way his confidence in God was soaring. Sometimes the tough relationships in our lives cause our confidence in God to grow!

DAY 19

Dangerous Relationship

In the spring, at the time when kings go off to war, David sent
Joab out with the king's men and the whole Israelite army.
They destroyed the Ammonites and besieged Rabbah.
But David remained in Jerusalem.
2 SAMUEL 11:1

Perhaps that's where the problem began. David wasn't where
he was supposed to be. The scripture says that it was spring,
"the time when kings [went] off to war." So why did David
stay home? He was king, and he was a warrior. He belonged
on the battlefield, but he stayed back.

Often when we're not where we're supposed to be, trouble
happens. The Bible tells us that David was a man after God's
own heart (see Acts 13:22). David had lots of God confidence. Yet even so, David found himself at the wrong place
at the wrong time.

He strolled outside onto his balcony, and across the way
he saw his neighbor Bathsheba taking a bath on *her* balcony.
Right then, David could have made an extremely smart move
by turning away and going back inside. But he lingered. He
watched. He fantasized. Finally, the fantasy became reality.
This is the progression of sin.

The apostle James outlines this progression in James

1:13–16: "Remember, when someone wants to do wrong it is never God who is tempting him, for God never wants to do wrong and never tempts anyone else to do it. Temptation is the pull of man's own evil thoughts and wishes. These evil thoughts lead to evil actions and afterwards to the death penalty from God. So don't be misled, dear brothers" (TLB).

David's sin could have been avoided if he had leaned on his confidence in God to direct his footsteps back inside or to the battlefield where he belonged. But he ignored his God confidence and allowed himself to sin. David had Bathsheba brought to the palace and had sexual relations with her. When she became pregnant, he brought her husband home from the battlefield for a short break. David assumed Uriah would sleep with his wife, and when he found out she was pregnant, he would think the child was his.

But Uriah chose not to sleep with Bathsheba out of respect for his men on the battlefield. "If they can't have the comfort, warmth, and privilege of being with their wives, why should I?" he asked David.

So the king went even further in his sin and had Uriah placed on the front line of battle to ensure his death. After Uriah's death David took Bathsheba as his wife. It's obvious that the king was becoming very comfortable with dysfunction. If we had time to trace his entire life, we'd see that the dysfunction began years ago. We don't have time in this space to look at his life that closely, but we can view a few examples of his dysfunction.

Years earlier David took multiple women as his wives. Though this was culturally accepted, it was never right in God's sight (see Deuteronomy 17:17). This dysfunction in David's household resulted in numerous children and step-children. His daughter Tamar was raped by her half brother Amnon. We know that David was a great warrior on the battlefield but was terrible at handling conflict off the field. He swept the situation under the carpet.

Years later, when David's son Absalom tried to remove his father from the throne, David reacted again in a manner that reflected his dysfunction. He had tremendous God confidence, yet he didn't always have a good track record of using it when he should have. And in spite of that, God still called David a man after His own heart.

This should give us hope! When we find ourselves in a tempting situation or a relationship that's not right, we need to remember to use our confidence in God. He has the ability and the desire to help us escape temptation.

Here's the proof: "But remember this—the wrong desires that come into your life aren't anything new and different. Many others have faced exactly the same problems before you. And no temptation is irresistible. You can trust God to keep the temptation from becoming so strong that you can't stand up against it, for he has promised this and will do what he says. He will show you how to escape temptation's power so that you can bear up patiently against it" (1 Corinthians 10:13 TLB).

God will empower us—through His Holy Spirit—to be victorious if we'll let Him.

We know David didn't rely on God to help him escape temptation; he gave in to it.

But God wasn't finished with David. Even after David has blown it (he has committed adultery and is responsible for Uriah's death), God still has plans for him. He uses Nathan the prophet to confront David with his sin. David is teachable, humble, and truly broken. He confesses and repents, and God forgives him. Now restored, he once again begins to depend on his God confidence.

We need to remember that God will always forgive a truly repentant heart (see 1 John 2:1). But in the Greek language, the word we translate "repent" actually means "to turn completely away from." So to pray a flippant prayer such as, "Sorry about that, God," and inside our hearts plan to repeat the sin is not true repentance.

God knows our hearts. But if we choose to continue to rebel against what we know God has forbidden, we're not depending on our God confidence to help us escape temptation, and we're setting the stage for our hearts to become hardened. A hardened heart becomes so comfortable with sin that it no longer feels the need to repent and is incapable of hearing God's tender voice.

Ask God to multiply your confidence in Him and to teach you to *depend* on that confidence so that you will follow His escape plan when you find yourself in a tempting situation or a wrong relationship.

DAY 20
That's Our Son!

"Be still, and know that I am God."
PSALM 46:10 ESV

Marcia's biggest test of faith has been with her middle son, Andrew. "It seems as though his life is usually. . .just. . .hanging in the balance!" she says. "My husband, Steve, and I constantly remind him that he's not a cat, and he won't have nine lives! He's a wonderful young adult now and has apologized for the grief he has put us through."

Andrew was colicky as a baby and had more ear infections than his brother and sister put together. He seemed to always question what his parents told him to do, and they easily got frustrated with him. His dad, Steve, is a large, tall, athletic man. Steve's high school football team won state, and he took second place in the state wrestling finals. Andrew is a much smaller guy and often easily evaded the sight of his parents.

The family vacationed to NASA in Houston and was seated on the ground watching and listening to a lecture about stars when Andrew somehow disappeared through the crowd to look for the space shuttle. "NASA had to lock down the entire facility until we found Andrew," Marcia says. "On trips like these, we always wore brightly colored matching shirts as a family so we could easily locate Andrew if we lost him. But somehow he still got away.

"My parents and grandparents have always had a strong faith," Marcia says, "and they've lifted countless prayers for Steve and me—and Andrew. My dad was a great people watcher, and he understood human nature like no one else. He and Andrew also had a lot in common, so it seemed they had a natural connection. Whenever we couldn't find him, Daddy always said, 'Think like Andrew.'"

Another time the family went to an outdoor drama called *The Man Who Ran*—the story of the Old Testament prophet Jonah. Before the drama began, they enjoyed an outdoor dinner with the other attendees. "Andrew wanted to wear roller skates," Marcia says. "My mom thought it might be a good idea because the skates were noisy, and we'd be able to keep up with him better.

"The skates did slow him down a bit—until he went downhill on a sidewalk with a curve at the bottom and broke his arm. It was simply one thing after another!" Marcia says.

"Steve and I are both solid Christians, and though it was taxing and exhausting with Andrew, our confidence in God actually grew stronger. He had to be our strength."

The biggest test with Andrew came during a beautiful Oklahoma day when Marcia's dad took the grandkids to his ranch to fish. "The fish weren't biting, so they decided to mow around the barn and get ready for a Sunday school party that would be held there in the evening," Marcia says.

The boys climbed on top of the tractor as their grandfather attached the mower. To his surprise, Andrew engaged the tractor, and it started to roll. Marcia's dad yelled at the boys to hang on, but Andrew thought he said to jump off. Andrew jumped, and the tractor tire ran over his head. As the tractor kept rolling, Grandpa ran to the front of the vehicle to turn it off, but the tractor knocked him down. He immediately began praying and says that angels must have picked him up before the tire ran over his legs. He quickly ran back to the tractor and was able to reach over and turn it off.

"Many miracles happened that day," Marcia says. "It had been a wet spring, so Andrew's head was squished against the soft, wet soil as the tire ran over him. That helped to serve as a cushion, but there was a chance this type of injury could cause him to have seizures."

Grandpa scooped the bleeding Andrew into his arms and drove the boys to the hospital. Miraculously, he was able to get Andrew to the hospital in time for medication to be administered that decreased the swelling in his brain and kept it from killing him.

"The best neurosurgeon in the state was leaving the hospital as we were walking inside. After seeing a nurse run after him, I remember hearing him call his wife to tell her he was going into surgery," Marcia says. "What a miracle that he would happen to be there—at this specific hospital!"

This happened to be a Wednesday evening, so many friends were already at church nearby, and they came to sit and pray with the family as Andrew underwent surgery. "These people had such strong God confidence," Marcia remembers. "And their confidence strengthened our confidence!"

There were tractor marks across Andrew's chest, but he had no severely damaged body parts. He had some shattered bones and a depressed skull that had to be cleaned.

A week later Andrew's stitches were removed. He passed all the physical therapy tests, and he never had a seizure. "The words of an old hymn kept repeating in my mind," Marcia says: " 'On Christ the solid rock I stand, all other ground is sinking sand.'

"As I mentioned earlier, Andrew is an adult now, and we no longer have to worry about keeping up with him, losing him, or wondering what's going to happen next. His own God confidence will carry him through," Marcia says.

GOD CONFIDENCE WHEN THE UNEXPECTED HAPPENS

DAY 21

Embracing Hope When Life Hurts

*Is your life full of difficulties and temptations? Then be happy,
for when the way is rough, your patience has a chance to grow.
So let it grow, and don't try to squirm out of your problems.
For when your patience is finally in full bloom, then you will
be ready for anything, strong in character, full and complete.*
JAMES 1:2–4 TLB

Last summer—right after she came home from experiencing the spiritual high of church camp—Denise experienced the sudden loss of her forty-seven-year-old brother, Davie. "He was an alcoholic," she says. "I prayed and prayed for years and never saw him get saved. He had been drinking and climbed onto a large lawn mower and started to drive. It soon tipped over into a fifteen-foot ditch and crushed him."

Denise was brokenhearted over the fact that she didn't know where her brother would spend eternity. "I hoped and hoped that he had prayed before he died. I know if he had simply called on the name of Jesus, that Jesus would have saved his soul. But I just didn't know."

Denise knelt at the place where Davie died, and she cried out to God. "I didn't know how I'd continue to live with the loss of my brother and with not knowing where he was spending eternity," she says.

While praying, Denise heard God's voice. *"Do you trust Me, Denise? Do you love Me?"*

"I answered, 'Yes, Lord. I love You with all my heart. And I *do* trust You.'"

"I'm the only One who knows where your brother is. Leave it with Me. Trust Me."

Denise was able to leave the issue with God right there. "He gave me His indescribable peace," she says, "and He restored my confidence in Him. I've been at peace over my brother ever since that moment. And I have more confidence in God today than I ever have before. I know my Redeemer lives, and He is trustworthy!"

Just three years earlier, Denise's mom died. "She was my best friend," Denise says. "She had an aneurysm that eventually took her life seven months later."

After the death of her mom, both of Denise's grandparents passed away, her dog died, and then Davie was gone. To add to the grief, two of Denise's siblings are in jail.

"I lost weight, lost my joy, lost my sense of humor, lost friends, lost a sense of reality, lost my self-worth. . .maybe it was because the grief hit me so fast and so hard that I just didn't know how to handle it all. I pulled back from people and became distant."

But God didn't leave Denise in that dark spot. Through it all, He made His presence known. "Even when I felt I had hit rock bottom, I felt Him," she says. "I know God was with me.

And He was building back my confidence in Him."

During the darkest moments in our lives, if we have a relationship with Christ, we can still cling to the *fact* that we have heaven waiting for us! "There's a lot I don't understand," Denise says. "But there's one thing I know for sure. The same Jesus who saved me and forgave my sins when I was eight years old, and the same Jesus who has set me apart for His glory, is the same Jesus who has never left me and who has always loved me.

"He has been intimately near to me through every painful moment of the unexpected. He is speaking, teaching, and patiently helping me laugh and love again."

DAY 22

The Day My Life Turned Upside Down

Yea, though I walk through the valley of the shadow of death,
I will fear no evil: for thou art with me; thy rod and thy staff they
comfort me. Thou preparest a table before me in the presence of mine
enemies: thou anointest my head with oil; my cup runneth over.
Surely goodness and mercy shall follow me all the days of my life:
and I will dwell in the house of the LORD for ever.
PSALM 23:4–6 KJV

It was Mother's Day when Kelly's water broke. She and her husband, Tim, were expecting their second child. They had already chosen a name: Tyler Scott Burlington. Labor began early in the day, and she and Tim headed for the hospital.

At 3:09 p.m. Tyler was born. But the day meant for celebration suddenly turned into excruciating grief. "Our son died the day he was born due to heart failure caused by a chromosomal condition called trisomy 18," Kelly says. "We only had two hours to hold our son, take photos, and sing to him. Tyler looked like Tim with his distinctive chin, high cheekbones, and straight nose."

The physician and hospital staff were compassionate and thoughtful toward the young couple. "Our family and church friends were also an incredible support," Kelly says. "I was twenty-seven years old, and I felt myself slipping into a horrible darkness—something I had never imagined.

"I think every mother worries that something terrible could happen to her child, but I never truly felt I would have to face the death of *my* child."

The next year was the most difficult time Kelly had ever experienced. Oftentimes she would have remained in bed if it hadn't been for their eighteen-month-old daughter, Emily. Kelly continued to meet Emily's needs, care for her, love her, and comfort her.

"But there were days when I cried nonstop," Kelly says. "And there were times I just got explosively angry. I didn't think life would ever get better again."

Kelly's husband was pastoring a church full of people who were trying to reach out to their pastor's wife, but they didn't know the depth of her depression and sometimes felt helpless.

"But after a year," Kelly says, "in the midst of my darkness, cracks began to appear and light slowly started to shine through. I knew God was speaking love to me. I knew He was asking me to trust Him.

"In the deepest human pain I had ever known, I felt a comfort and peace begin to overtake the sadness and despair. God's presence and love became a reality for me," she says. "My confidence in my Redeemer was returning.

"I can't adequately put into words how God changed my life as I grieved for my son. It may sound strange, but the most difficult time for me emotionally became the most special time for me spiritually!"

Kelly refused to let the despair and depression win. Her marriage became stronger, her outlook on life grew more grateful, and she developed a more patient style of parenting.

God was providing a crown of beauty instead of ashes, the oil of gladness instead of mourning, and a garment of praise instead of despair (see Isaiah 61:3). That's a miracle!

So why would Kelly want to think about, speak about, and write about a depressing time in her life?

"First, it's therapeutic for me. Second, life is tough for everyone. Whether it's death, divorce, devastating news, or even the difficulties of daily life, there's nothing that can defeat us!

"If we'll put our faith in God, He will rush to meet us at our exact point of need. He is close to the brokenhearted! He rescues those who feel crushed in their spirit. Christ saved me from living the rest of my life in darkness and hopelessness.

"This is what I've learned from the brief life of my son: Hope is a beautiful thing. Faith gives strength. And love that comes from God can defeat any darkness or fear!"

DAY 23

One Adventure after Another

So, my dear brothers, since future victory is sure,
be strong and steady, always abounding in the Lord's work.
1 CORINTHIANS 15:58 TLB

Rachel gave her heart to Christ when she was a little girl, so her God confidence has been growing for several years. "He has always been so faithful and kind to me," she says. "When I was just fourteen years old, I felt God's call to missions."

Most of Rachel's family members are dedicated Christians, but none of them is in full-time ministry, so this announcement from a teenager was hard for them to accept. After all, she could certainly be a strong Christian and serve God in a variety of places like millions of others do. But full-time ministry?

"My announcement was simply shrugged off," Rachel says, "and everyone assumed I'd go to college and become a teacher or a writer. And after a while, I even started to buy into that. It's what made sense."

Rachel's dad works at the state university, so tuition for her would be free. "I attended my first year there and was miserable," she says. "It wasn't because I didn't like the school or the subject matter; it just didn't feel right to me. I knew there had to be more."

Her parents couldn't help but notice how unhappy she was and told her that she could apply to some ministry schools. But they told her she could only attend if one of those other colleges could give her a full scholarship since she could attend college for free by staying local.

"This seemed impossible to me," Rachel says. "My grades were good, but my test scores weren't full-ride material. Still, in the midst of the doubt, I could feel God working and adding to the faith I already had. It was exciting!"

Rachel began her search, and by April of her freshman year, she stumbled on Central Bible College in Springfield, Missouri. "I'd heard of it," she says, "but I honestly never considered it. After all, Missouri was a long way from my home state of Ohio. But my God confidence began to grow."

As she viewed their scholarship page, she read that one full scholarship was given each year to incoming students. She grinned when she noticed that her test scores were good enough to qualify her for application.

"Time was running out," Rachel says. "I only had a couple of weeks to apply for the school and the scholarship. I was scared. I had no idea what I was getting myself into, but God assured me that He was in this."

She prayed over the envelope containing her application before dropping it into the mailbox. "I told Jesus that I wanted to be in the center of His will. My utmost desire was obedience," Rachel says.

Deep in her heart, she had decided that she'd move to Springfield and attend CBC no matter what, but she prayed that God would touch her parents' hearts and move them to know this was His will.

"I knew that without this scholarship there would be a lot of stress on my family, a lot of arguments, and a lot of debt. I didn't want that, but I knew beyond doubt God was in this. I couldn't turn away from it."

Though Rachel thought it seemed highly unlikely she'd get the scholarship, she continued to pray for the sake of her parents. During Fourth of July weekend—less than a month before she would be moving—Rachel received a phone call from an administrator informing her that she had been chosen for the scholarship.

"I cried on the phone with him," she says. "I was so overwhelmed at God's goodness! He had heard and answered my prayer. Not only would I attend debt-free, but I'd be in an environment conducive to missions work, and He had provided confirmation for my family.

"I felt God was telling me and my family once and for all that He had called me and we were never to question that again," she says. "And *because* He has called, He will be faithful to meet my needs. *My* responsibility," Rachel says, "is to trust, obey, and follow even when the steps are risky and don't seem to make sense."

A few years later, Rachel moved to Seattle—without a

car, a job, or a place to live—to help with a church plant. Within a month, she had secured a job as a nanny with a family that has become like a second family to her. "More than once, God has provided all I've needed in His perfect timing," she says.

Three months from now, Rachel will move to Guadalajara, Mexico, to teach preschool. "Again, this is completely out of my comfort zone," she says, "but I have total God confidence that He's in charge.

"This is the joy and beauty of life lived with Christ! It's one big, wonderful adventure. We don't always get to see what's coming next, but He is so faithful and kind and good to us. With every crazy step of faith we take, we get to see more of His character. The adventure continues to unfold as we keep our God confidence strong—even though we don't always know which direction we're headed next. My life with Him is far more amazing than what I ever could have planned on my own!"

That's the result of God confidence.

DAY 24
Unexpected Behavior

But the fruit of the Spirit is love, joy, peace, forbearance, kindness, goodness, faithfulness, gentleness and self-control.
GALATIANS 5:22–23

Troy has been a Christian for five years, and even though he has memorized the list of the fruit of the Spirit mentioned in today's scripture, often there are times he doesn't experience peace. There are also times he argues simply for the sake of arguing. Let's put Troy on pause for a moment. We'll come back to him after we take a closer look at the fruit of the Spirit.

As your relationship with Christ grows, the Holy Spirit will begin developing special fruit (as mentioned in today's scripture) in your life. This is another "mark of ownership" from God. As this fruit is manifested and multiplied in your life, it serves as a witness to those around you that you belong to God. Again, think of the branding of JESUS on your forehead. (See Day 5.) The fruit of the Holy Spirit matches that branding.

But think about this: You won't automatically become the world's most patient person simply because you're a Christian and patience is a fruit of the Spirit. The Holy Spirit *develops* this fruit in your life, and that's a process. Think of actual fruit growing on a tree. It doesn't appear as soon as you plant the seed. Nor does this fruit of the Spirit appear as soon as you accept Christ as your Savior.

But as you water an apple seedling, it will eventually become a tree. It requires sun, water, and great care, however, to become a tree. And once it's a tree, bearing fruit still doesn't happen immediately. Again, it's a process. But finally, you'll see the apple on the branch of your tree, and you'll rejoice at the final product.

To grow spiritually, you require the Son's nourishment. This comes from the Bible, the Holy Spirit, corporate worship, and accountability. As you mature in your faith, the fruit of the Spirit becomes evidenced in your lifestyle.

Does this mean that *all* of the fruit of the Spirit will always be evident in your life all the time? No. But when you're not experiencing peace, for example, you can quickly discover why. There's an extremely important paragraph of scripture *before* today's passage that will show you why you're not experiencing a specific fruit of the Spirit. Let's take a look:

"The acts of the flesh are obvious: sexual immorality, impurity and debauchery; idolatry and witchcraft; hatred, discord, jealousy, fits of rage, selfish ambition, dissensions, factions and envy; drunkenness, orgies, and the like. I warn you, as I did before, that those who live like this will not inherit the kingdom of God" (Galatians 5:19–21).

You wonder why you're not experiencing peace? Use this paragraph as a checklist. Read through the acts of the flesh and find the one you're currently struggling with. For example, if you're displaying anger (fits of rage), that explains why you're not experiencing peace.

When we're not enjoying the fruit of the Spirit, it's because something in the above paragraph (an act of the flesh) has canceled it out. You're no longer joyful? Go through the above list. It could be due to the fact that jealousy has canceled out your joy. You're not loving others as you should? Are you envious of someone? Acting hateful toward someone?

It's exciting how God's Word not only can help us grow closer to Him but also can guide us into becoming more like Him!

We'll push the PLAY button now and get back to Troy. When he's being argumentative, it's common sense that he won't be engaged in peaceful actions. For Troy to exemplify peace, he needs to discipline himself to stop arguing with others. Accountability with another person would be a great help. And continued prayer will also help.

Troy doesn't need to continue with unexpected behavior with the acts of the flesh. He can surrender *all* of his life to the *lordship* of Jesus Christ and learn to live in the power of the Holy Spirit. Once we live, act, and react in His power, our God confidence soars.

Perhaps you've already asked God to forgive your sins,

but like Troy, you're not really living in the power of the Holy Spirit. Maybe the fruit of His Spirit is rarely evident in your life. Here's a prayer that can guide you into this kind of commitment. Again, like the prayer given on Day 1, these aren't magic words. You can pray your own prayer. The issue is simply to mean it from your heart!

> Dear Jesus, thank You for forgiving my sins. Thank You that I'm a Christian. But as I'm trying to live a holy life, I realize I can't do it in my own strength. I need Your power. I want the fruit of Your Spirit evidenced in my life. Will You sanctify me? Cleanse me within and remove everything in my life that's not of You. Release the power of Your Spirit within me, and teach me how to live a holy life in Your power. As I grow in You, continue to increase my God confidence. Amen.

DAY 25

Diabetic but Confident

*Now faith is confidence in what we hope
for and assurance about what we do not see.*
HEBREWS 11:1

Beth has been a type 1 diabetic since the age of seven, and she's now sixty. "I've learned that no insulin equals no life," she says. "I'm extremely careful to follow my physician's instructions, and I'm consistent to take the medicine I need without varying the dosage. My body needs a very specific amount, so I don't deviate from what has been prescribed.

"I live in Dennison, Ohio, but I receive my insulin from Canada because it's a lot less expensive than buying it here in the States."

Because Beth doesn't have insurance, the cost of her medicine is $500 for two vials of insulin if purchased at a pharmacy in her area. By ordering it from Canada, however, she gets four vials for $525.

Beth's husband was working in Alaska, and she was scheduled to see him on the weekend. When she received the tracking number for her insulin on Monday, she realized there would be a dilemma in getting the medicine she needed at the time she needed it.

"The tracking showed that I wouldn't get the insulin until

Friday, but there was no set time as to when the mail carrier in our small town would deliver my package. I wasn't going to be home much of the day—lunch with my parents in a neighboring town and time with friends—so I knew I had a major problem with my schedule and the delivery of my medicine."

Beth began praying in the wee hours of the morning, asking God to bring her insulin early in the day on Friday. "Besides my body going into shock, the other consequence of not receiving the insulin was that because it was coming from another country, the postal service had the right to throw it away if I wasn't present at delivery time, and I wouldn't be able to get reimbursed."

As Beth prayed, she sensed God challenging her. *Do you believe I answer all prayers? Small prayers as well as big prayers? Simple requests as well as complicated ones?*

"I knew my prayer was a mix," she says. "Asking God to bring my mail early was a simple request, but the consequences I would experience if I didn't receive it before my get-together with my husband were quite complicated."

Beth has been a Christian for years and has watched her faith deepen through the decades. "I've seen God work in my life several times," she says. "He has answered too many prayers for me to count, and He has always met my needs. So because He has a perfect track record, you'd think it would be easy to always trust, right?"

Beth never doubted God's ability for a second; she knew He could send an angel with her meds if He wanted to. "But I did worry about the system," she says. "I had full confidence in God, but I was unsure about our postal service. As I continued to pray, though, God reminded me that He has control over everything and can even intervene in the postal service."

Beth's insulin was delivered before she left the house on Friday, and she was able to enjoy time with her husband without any concern. God cares about every detail in our lives! His timing is always perfect.

There's nothing too small to pray about, and there's nothing too big to pray about. If it concerns you, it concerns your heavenly Father. He is so concerned about every detail in your life that He even knows the exact number of hairs on your head—at this very moment (see Luke 12:7)!

We're told in Philippians 4:6 to pray about *everything*. God wants us to give Him our concerns. Why is this important? Because prayer dissipates worry. The more you pray, the less you worry. Prayer also acts as a bonding agent. It cements you closer to your heavenly Father. And when that happens? Your God confidence deepens!

GOD CONFIDENCE HELPS US THROUGH HEALTH CRISES

DAY 26

The "Widow Maker"

*Now faith is confidence in what we hope
for and assurance about what we do not see.*
HEBREWS 11:1

November 14, 2014, could have been a major game changer in life as Dennis and Charlene knew it. Dennis enjoys teaching art at the local high school—as well as serving as senior pastor for the local Nazarene church in Anderson, Missouri. This was the date he was scheduled for surgery.

Six months earlier, Dennis noticed an unrelenting tightness in his chest. He had a few appointments with the doctor and even made two trips to the emergency room, but he was misdiagnosed with chondritis—inflammation in the chest wall. It was only when his blood pressure skyrocketed when he went to the ER a final time and the doctor assigned a stress test that the professionals began to see the danger Dennis was in.

He was scheduled for bypass surgery to correct two heart blockages. "Doctors had told me that my veins were 100 and 90 percent blocked," Dennis says.

"You can imagine my concern—knowing that the vein nicknamed the 'widow maker' was 90 percent blocked," his wife, Charlene, says.

She couldn't hold her tears inside during dinner that evening. Dennis put his fork down, looked his wife in the eyes, and said, "Charlene, God is going to give me exactly what's best for me."

Those words greatly comforted Charlene. To hear of her husband's confidence in God helped strengthen her own faith. "He didn't tell me that he had heard from God, that he would make it through surgery, and that God was going to heal him," Charlene says. "But what he did tell me was that God was in charge."

"As I prayed about the situation," Dennis says, "God clearly revealed to me that He was in control and that I would be okay either way. So I was confident in what He had told me."

The couple had been married for thirty-three years when Dennis went into the four-hour surgery. "Seeing and hearing his God confidence as he was wheeled into the operating room gave me the confidence that God would take care of us," Charlene says.

"I realize that there's a deeper level of confidence that comes when we release the care of our future into the hands of our Creator. Of course, oftentimes in situations like this, God chooses to take us home to be with Him. We must be okay with His will—whether it means continued life on earth or life in heaven."

The surgery was successful, and Dennis continues to schedule regular checkups. He also keeps teaching and preaching with passion and excellence.

DAY 27

That Phone Call from the Doctor

I write these things to you who believe in the name of the Son of God so that you may know that you have eternal life.
1 JOHN 5:13

Sheri's husband, Rick, had just retired after thirty-seven years as a meteorologist, and they were anticipating being empty nesters and enjoying the golden years. One month later, however, she discovered a lump in her breast. "It was very superficial," she says, "so I wasn't really worried, but I scheduled a mammogram."

Afterward, Sheri received a call to go back to the doctor's office for an ultrasound. "As the tech was doing the ultrasound procedure, she said, 'Oh, I see it. That's a cyst.' I was so relieved to hear those words—until I realized that she wasn't scanning the area where I had seen the lump. It was more of a bump—you could actually see it."

Sheri showed the tech what she felt, even though it hadn't shown up on the mammogram. The tech scanned that specific area and said it didn't look bad, but they'd do a biopsy anyway.

"They did a needle biopsy," Sheri says. "They used nine needles. The first needle bent inside my breast, so getting it out was a frustrating experience." The procedure was finally completed, and Sheri went home to wait for the news.

Just a few days later, on Tuesday, August 9, 2011, she got the phone call from her doctor that no one wants to receive. "I was told I had breast cancer. *Cancer*—the word that sticks to your tongue and echoes through your bones. One of my friends began weeping. Honestly, she was crying so hard, she was shaking. But from the very beginning," Sheri says, "I had such peace. I knew this kind of peace could only come from God. It was beyond description."

Sheri took her friend's hands, looked her in the eyes, and said, "My future is secure. I know where I'm going, and I'm trusting my God!"

The initial reports said the cancer was small, near the surface, and in only one breast. "So I had a lumpectomy—no other options were even suggested. The results showed that the lump was larger and deeper than they realized. And even worse news was to be had: the cancer had spread to my lymph nodes."

Sheri had a second surgery a week later because the margins weren't clear. After that surgery, she developed a staph infection. "Ugh! I was extremely frustrated, yet I felt God's strength in an undeniable way," she says.

"I had chemo for four months, and I followed that with two months of radiation. Though these treatments are necessary and often successful, they also leave one with no strength. I was extremely weak and tired."

But Sheri wasn't the only one hurting. The day after her last radiation treatment, her husband had triple bypass surgery!

"Remember, all this started after he retired," Sheri said. "We thought we'd be coasting down easy street and enjoying a life of relaxation, but instead we were both experiencing crucial health crises."

Six weeks later, Sheri's staph infection returned. She had to have surgery to clean out the infection. "The doctors had to leave the wound open because the radiated tissue wouldn't heal. We had to perform daily wound care for months," she says.

Sheri wore a wound vacuum for one month and spent two months going to daily hyperbaric chamber treatments. "But every single step of the way, I saw God's fingerprints," she says. "We have walked the cancer road with many people since then. Some have recovered. Some have passed on to eternity. But through it all, our God has been faithful."

Sheri sometimes wonders what would have happened if the Holy Spirit had not prompted her to speak up to the technician who was looking at a cyst instead of the actual cancer bump. "Things could have turned out much differently," she says. But her confidence in God remained strong and grew even stronger through the entire ordeal. "And because of this experience—as awful as it was—others now know about our God confidence," she says.

DAY 28
Six Time Zones Away (Part 1)

The LORD is my rock, my fortress and my deliverer;
my God is my rock, in whom I take refuge,
my shield and the horn of my salvation, my stronghold.
PSALM 18:2

"Veronica has always been full of surprises," Roberta says. "Since childhood she's been a bundle of energy, has loved life, and relishes travel. In fact, she turned fifteen up in the air one summer while on her very first mission trip to Poland and the Czech Republic."

Many more short-term mission trips followed in the next fifteen years. But the real surprise came when Veronica announced to her parents, John and Roberta, that she felt God was calling her into full-time missions work—six time zones away.

"She had a great job that she loved, so my first thought was, *But what about your dream job?* And then I thought about the realities, as moms do, and I asked how much it would pay and if it included medical insurance. She explained she'd be fund-raising and would have to get her own insurance."

Roberta's friends and extended family were concerned. "How can you let her go so far? And all alone?"

"Those who were believers understood the calling of God

on her life," Roberta says. "Others just watched, wondered, and stayed confused. Little did I know at the time that having her on the mission field would be the easier part of this upcoming journey."

For two years Veronica immersed herself into full-time fund-raising to join a missions team in Europe that would minister to teens. In January 2010 she visited Europe to apply for her visa. She was exhausted, and while there, she noticed that her glands were swollen.

"We just chalked it up to the stress of foreign language school and allergies," Roberta says.

When Veronica returned home the next month, she went to the doctor, and the doctor thought for sure it was mono. The following day she enrolled in missionary school. Later she had the mono test repeated as doctors suggested, but it came back negative again. She then came home to have a biopsy on the swollen nodules on her neck.

"John and I can now share with other parents of kids who are full-time missionaries that they are blessed if their children are healthy enough to remain on the mission field— even if it is six time zones away," Roberta says.

"Sitting in the oncologist's office was like sitting in the midst of a heavy fog. *Is this really happening? Is this for real?* The tests were back. Results were in. The doctor's words: 'Stage 4 non-Hodgkin's lymphoma. It's treatable, but it's not curable.'

"My thoughts and feelings just kept revolving around and around in my head," Roberta remembers. "It was hard to sleep because so much was on my mind. I was teaching second grade at the time, and my students would ask me if my daughter was going to die."

At the same time that Veronica was diagnosed with stage 4 cancer, the nursing home personnel where Roberta's father lived told her to call in hospice for him. "It was a daddy-daughter struggle!" Roberta says. "But I remembered that my Abba Daddy was with me every step of this nightmare. In fact, sometimes He just carried me.

"I was the mom. A mom takes care of her children, but I couldn't fix cancer! I couldn't just whip out a bandage and heal my little girl as I had done so many times in the past. I felt helpless. Thank God for God! I have no idea how people without Him handle tragedy. He was so close to our entire family and continued to remind us to keep our confidence in Him."

Roberta says there were two things she did that helped her during this journey. "A coworker gave me a 'praying cross' that fits into the palm of my hand. The ladies at her church prayed over it, and when I went to bed at night, I would hold it and also pray. It symbolizes that Jesus is holding on to me as I hold on to the cross. Many days all I could pray was His name. . .*Jesus*. I was confident He knew my heart, and He didn't need a lot of words."

The other thing Roberta did that kept her focused on God was to write down different Bible verses that reminded her that He was walking with her. She came to rest in the fact that she could trust His will for her daughter.

"One of the scriptures that God led me to was Psalm 112:7: 'He is not afraid of bad news; his heart is firm, trusting in the LORD' [ESV]. Other friends would text me verses, and I'd write them down. I had enough cards that I put a rubber band around them and carried the stack in my purse or coat pocket. They came in handy during chemo, tests, and just the everyday yuck of cancer."

As Roberta loosened her grip on Veronica, she was able to strengthen her grip on her heavenly Father, and her faith was continually deepened.

DAY 29

Six Time Zones Away (Part 2)

"For I am the LORD your God who takes hold of your right hand and says to you, Do not fear; I will help you."
ISAIAH 41:13

Veronica was finally in remission and able to complete her fund-raising! She moved to Europe to begin her mission journey with thirty-six crates filled with supplies, ministry materials, clothing, and furniture. She set up housekeeping, and her parents, John and Roberta, were able to see her apartment through Skype.

Veronica continued to receive chemo and PET scans while in Europe to maintain her remission. The doctors told her that her remission could last from five to ten years. And by then they hoped another form of treatment would be available, as there are wonderful advancements each year in cancer research. Veronica's remission, however, lasted only two years. She returned home.

"Once again my cross came out," Roberta says, "and my index cards grew deeper. I had retired, which was a blessing. I wondered what God was up to. A friend's little boy even asked, 'Why would God give a missionary cancer again? She was doing *His* work.'"

In spite of the fact that Veronica was on maintenance chemo, her cancer came back.

The cycle of more chemo began just after Veronica's hair had finally reached a nice length and once again had body and bounce to it. This second round of chemo didn't take her hair away but just thinned it a little.

After intense chemo for four months, Veronica was in her second remission. "This wasn't the end of treatment," Roberta says, "just a step in the even scarier ride of our lives. The doctors couldn't say how long this remission would last. They warned us that it might only be a few months."

After three years of different types of chemo, it was time for Veronica to have a stem cell transplant. A match was found, and almost two years ago she celebrated a new birthday! "It's been a bumpy ride," Roberta says, "but it's also been a ride worth taking."

Veronica is extremely active in her church and disciples several of the teens in the youth group. And after losing all her hair again during the transplant procedure, she's now enjoying getting haircuts!

"As her mom," Roberta says, "I would have taken the cancer away from Veronica and placed it on myself. But I wasn't given that choice. In spite of the roller coaster, I wouldn't want to remove the lessons I'm learning from this cancer journey."

Roberta looks at the cross in her hand. "I forget how hard

I held it, but it's looking rather battered. I'm reminded of Jesus and His cross and all the battering He took for you and me. Bottom line: He's got this. And He has me, too."

DAY 30

God Still Answers Prayer

And [Jesus] said, The things which are
impossible with men are possible with God.
LUKE 18:27 KJV

Grant graduated from a Christian university with a degree in science and planned on following his dad's and brother's career choice of teaching. He didn't have any trouble finding a job in a middle school only ten minutes from the university.

Grant loved teenagers and had served as a volunteer worker in the youth group at his local church. He enjoyed teaching science and watching the lightbulbs turn on in his students' eyes when they were successful at dissecting an earthworm or remembering specific minerals.

He grew up with a love for missions and prayed that his students would notice something different about his life. "I wanted my relationship with Christ to shine through my actions," he says. Once in a while a student would make a remark or ask a question that would allow Grant to open up to a limited degree about his faith.

Though he loved his job, Grant desired to share life's *real* answers with teens. He yearned to share more than science formulas. He wanted to share Christ with them and offer *eternal* solutions. So he began researching teaching in an international missions school.

"I didn't have much Bible training," he says. "I took the required religion classes at the Christian university I attended, and I knew the Bible, but I needed more to actually teach in a missions school."

Grant decided to take a break from teaching in the public school and attend a short-term missions school so he could gain what he lacked in biblical training. After that, he was commissioned by his church's denomination to serve as a missionary teacher at a Christian school for missionary kids in Europe.

"I was incredibly excited," he says. "This was a dream come true for me." Grant quickly made friends with several of the other single teachers at the school and enjoyed teaching science and leading a Bible study.

"Several times on weekends, I enjoyed traveling throughout other parts of the country, trying out the local cuisine, and visiting international-speaking churches. Even though I didn't understand the languages, I could always feel the presence of God, and I loved singing the same hymns and choruses we sang in the States."

Grant was finally able to encourage students in their walk with Christ as well as teach them the science skills they needed. "It was great to be able to pray with students, attend churches with them, and give devotions in their dorms," he says.

After teaching overseas for twelve years, Grant knew he had to make a decision. Should he continue teaching in a different culture, or should he return home and be closer to his aging parents? "After spending many nights in prayer, I sensed that God was telling me to go home," Grant says. "He revealed to me that He had brought me to Europe for a season, but now He wanted to use me back in the public school system again in the States."

It was extremely difficult to say good-bye to people who would now be lifetime friends, but Grant resigned and moved home. He returned to the same state he left—where his parents and siblings live and where he had attended college.

It didn't take him long to secure a teaching job in a public high school, and once again he began the process of loving students and teaching science. But not long after he returned home, he noticed something wasn't right healthwise.

"I had to go to the bathroom a lot," he says. "And I often had severe pain in my bladder."

He made several trips to a variety of doctors, and he was finally diagnosed with a rare disease called interstitial cystitis (IC for short). It's a difficult disease to diagnose because the symptoms can sometimes change from week to week. It means that the bladder is chronically inflamed.

Many people diagnosed with IC will have to urinate as often as forty, fifty, or sixty times a day, around the clock. The discomfort can be so excruciating and difficult to manage that only about half of those who have this disorder work full-time.

"There are some theories about the causes of IC, but no one really knows for sure," Grant says. "It was terrible. My life's routine had to change drastically. Obviously, because I'm single, I couldn't stop working or even just work part-time. I needed to continue teaching full-time."

He had to have a classroom near the restroom at school, and his social activities now revolved around the question of whether a bathroom would be near. For example, "I couldn't go water-skiing because I'd be in a boat for hours without access to a restroom. Same thing with snow skiing. Those are two sports I loved."

When he went to the movies with friends, he had to sit near an exit so he could frequent the bathroom during the movie. "And I couldn't even sit through an entire church service," Grant says. "I always had to sit near the back of our small sanctuary so I could easily get up and run to the bathroom and come back. It truly changed everything."

Grant began to pray for healing. "I've always had a close relationship with Christ," he says, "and I knew He could easily heal me. But I also know He sometimes chooses not to heal—like with the apostle Paul, who prayed and prayed for God to remove the thorn from his flesh. I didn't know if God would heal me or not, but my confidence was in Him! He had always provided for me in the past—my teaching jobs, my time in Europe, the house He enabled me to purchase. I made it a serious matter of prayer."

Grant also asked a few close friends to start praying as well. "It's not something I could share with a lot of people," he says, "because it's a very private disease. Obviously, it wasn't something I wanted to discuss."

Grant's family and a few friends began to pray consistently for his healing.

And then it happened.

One day Grant simply didn't have to go to the bathroom as much. And he wasn't experiencing any pain in his bladder. "I was almost scared to tell anyone about my good day," he says, "but I hoped and hoped it was a sign of my healing."

Several more normal days followed, and Grant has been free of IC for two years now. "My God confidence would have remained strong if He had chosen not to heal me," he says. "But I'm rejoicing that after praying for fourteen years, I've been healed and can live a normal life!"

GOD CONFIDENCE IN
THE MIDST OF LOSS

DAY 31

Something Beautiful? (Part 1)

The Lord is close to the brokenhearted
and saves those who are crushed in spirit.
Psalm 34:18

Greg and his wife, Hannah, had been in pastoral ministry for eighteen years when they received a call to a church in another state away from their family. "After seeking God's direction," Greg says, "we both felt His clear confirmation that we should move. So we obeyed."

"We made friends in our new church—people whom we quickly trusted and with whom we shared good times," Hannah says. "Things went well for the first three years, but then things began to change."

Many in the church began to pull away from Pastor Greg's desire to reach the community. They were comfortable with the way things were and didn't mind settling for the status quo.

"Some of our 'friends' got together and decided they no longer wanted us there," Hannah says. "They carefully strategized their ambush. Ensuing board meetings were planned and held. Greg asked them to pray about their decision, but their minds were already made up. They wanted us gone."

Pastor Greg and Hannah stayed for the next four weeks as promised in their resignation, and then they were gone. Though they were unaware of the planned ambush, they had recently asked a Realtor to evaluate their home for the possibility of selling it.

"One night Hannah arrived home from work, and I told her about the ambush," Greg remembers. "So we immediately decided to call the Realtor and put a sign in the front yard. God sold our home in three days with a cash buyer."

"The next nine months were full of agony, hurt, fear, loneliness, and a mix of negative feelings," Hannah admits. "I was very confused—and even angry at times—because of God's seemingly silent presence in our circumstances. I couldn't understand why God would lead us so far from home then allow things to change so drastically. I felt betrayed by our friends. And unfortunately, we had to remain in the same area as our former church because of my job."

Both Hannah and Greg spent each morning in prayer. "But I was struggling with so many troubled feelings," Hannah says. "I couldn't understand what had happened. Why wouldn't Christians want to grow their church? Why wouldn't they desire to become all that God wanted for them?"

Hannah simply continued to pray without understanding. "I read my Bible and copied scripture verses inside my journal that were helpful for me during those days.

"I struggled a lot with anxiety because, as a woman, I needed to know where my 'nest' would be—and if we could afford it. I somehow knew that God would take care of us, but I also wanted to know where and how that would happen."

About nine months later, Greg received a call that a particular church was going to open and his name would be presented to them. "We were excited," Hannah says, "and I viewed that as a way to end my anxiety."

But the next call Greg got was to tell him that this new church wanted to interview someone else—someone younger. "I felt as if my heart fell from my chest," Greg says. "And Hannah cried herself to sleep."

Obeying God doesn't mean exemption from trials, nor does it mean that obedience is easy. Often obedience is the hardest thing we do, but we do it because we're committed to Him. Christ obeyed His Father all the way to the cross. It surely wasn't easy.

We sometimes think that because we're doing what God has told us to do, it shouldn't be hard. We read an amazing description of what it was like for the disciples to battle a raging storm at sea in Matthew 14:22–33. They had been crossing the Sea of Galilee since evening. Darkness had fallen, and they were rowing against the wind.

Most boats had sails, but we are told that the disciples were rowing. A sail wouldn't have helped in this storm anyway. Their boat was just too small, and the waves were too big. These disciples were pretty sure they wouldn't make it to dawn. They believed this was their final chapter.

Why were they in a boat at night? Because earlier in the evening Jesus *told* them to get in the boat and cross the sea. About 3:00 a.m., they saw what they believed to be a ghost—and it was walking on the water toward them!

These men were already physically and mentally exhausted. Now they were terrified. But Jesus shouted His identity to them and calmed their fears—as well as the waves. The disciples could have said, "Lord, why are we in this storm? We're only doing what You told us to do! We're simply being obedient. So why has this been so difficult? So exhausting?"

Jesus replaced their fear and exhaustion with solid God confidence. And He'll do that for you, too! When you find yourself fighting storms in the midst of obedience, look up. You'll always see Jesus right in front of you.

Greg and Hannah kept looking up.

DAY 32

Something Beautiful? (Part 2)

*Those who know your name trust in you, for you,
LORD, have never forsaken those who seek you.*
PSALM 9:10

"Again, I was excited about the possibility of another church being interested in us and giving us a place to belong," Hannah says. "We were broken, lonely, confused, and hurting deeply. We just wanted to minister, and couldn't understand why it was so hard to simply do God's will."

A few weeks later, Greg received another call stating that the younger pastor turned the church down, and they wanted to interview him.

Greg and Hannah went through the interviewing process, and this new church family extended an invitation to Greg to be their pastor.

"It was extremely difficult to see God's hand through those nine months—especially while we walked through the process of leaving the last church," Greg says. "But our new church turned out to be a perfect match regarding our needs and our gifts."

God gave Greg and Hannah a new church family and a new set of true friends. "I can't imagine living life without them," Hannah says. "Looking back over that year, God was with us each step of the way. He took care of us through each hurdle of those nine long months. God knew I struggled with anxiety, so He gave me two jobs that kept me very busy so I didn't have much time to worry about the future.

"He also gave me a very supportive Christian boss who helped me through my daily tasks by praying *for* me and *with* me. I later discovered that my boss even supplemented my salary simply because he knew we needed it."

Hannah sees those difficult months as a time of growing closer to Greg and closer to God. "Greg didn't work during that time," she says. "I was thankful God gave me the two jobs to fill my time and to allow my husband to genuinely rest for a while.

"My daily times of prayer gave me a peace that assured me God would take care of us even though I didn't know how it would end. Though I questioned, and though I hurt deeply, my confidence in God was strong and surprisingly growing even stronger."

As Hannah looks back, she can now see God's handprint on every single step of their nine-month journey. "I learned to trust Him even when He was silent," she says. "I learned that when He seems silent, He's really there—consistently meeting our needs and taking care of details for our future."

"This difficult period of our lives has taught me to trust my heavenly Father even more," Greg says. "He has given me a peace like no other, both during and after the difficult times."

Hannah had a hard time forgiving the "friends" from their former church. "I made the conscious choice to forgive, but I know I'll never forget," she says. "Forgiveness doesn't mean that I'll forget the nine-month ordeal. I never want to forget God's blessings during that difficult time.

"The very act of forgiving implies that something was done that was wrong. Forgiveness is a choice that only I can choose. And I choose to forgive because God tells me to. . .and because He has chosen to forgive *me*. I choose to obey Him. I *needed* to forgive so I wouldn't continue to carry the burden around.

"Forgiving doesn't mean that I'm obligated to tell the other person/church that I forgive them. *I* am the prisoner that God released from prison when I chose to forgive them. He truly freed me from hanging on to the hurtful burdens and memories. My God confidence has soared, and I can see how He really does make something beautiful out of pain."

Let's flash back once again to the disciples in the midst of the storm at sea. Right before they got in the boat to cross the Sea of Galilee, they had witnessed Jesus multiply bread and fish for a crowd of approximately twenty thousand (if we counted the men, women, and children). They were on a spiritual high! They were mentally stretched because they had just witnessed a miracle. Bread and fish were multiplied before their eyes!

After this miracle, the people left to go home. Jesus told

the disciples to get in their boat and cross the sea while He went farther up into the mountains to pray. He wanted some alone time with Father God.

It's often after a spiritual high that we experience great struggle. In fact, we can learn to plan ahead for it. After God blesses you in a wonderful way, get out your Bible and put on your spiritual armor, because Satan will be right around the corner ready to pounce. He'll throw darts of doubt at you or plant seeds of doubt in those around you—as he did in Greg and Hannah's story.

While God was doing wonderful things in their first church, a storm was brewing. We expect storms from the world, but when they come from those within the church, we're hurt doubly hard.

The apostle Paul told Timothy that there will come a time when those in the church turn against the truth being taught (see 1 Timothy 4:1–2). When it happens, look up. Jesus is with you. He can make something beautiful from the deepest pain. And He's always ready to restore your God confidence.

DAY 33

We Lost. . .and We Gained

"Bring the whole tithe into the storehouse, that there may be food in my house. Test me in this," says the LORD Almighty, "and see if I will not throw open the floodgates of heaven and pour out so much blessing that there will not be room enough to store it."
MALACHI 3:10

Early in her marriage, Josie began hearing about tithing. "My husband and I decided on a church to attend, and the pastor often preached about the importance of giving God what was His," she says.

"This was a new concept for us. Neither one of us came from Christian backgrounds, and we had no idea what tithing meant or why it was important."

The more they listened to their new pastor and read the Bible, they discovered that God asks His children to faithfully give 10 percent of what they earn to the "storehouse"—the church. Without tithes and offerings, it would be impossible for God's church to exist—let alone grow or expand in outreach ministry.

God soon began dealing with Josie and her husband about tithing. "We were on a very tight budget," she says. "How could we afford to lose money by giving it to the church? We just didn't have 10 percent to give."

But the more they prayed about it, the more they were convinced God was revealing to them that tithing was an act of obedience. "We definitely wanted to obey God," Josie says. "Both of us prayed about it and just stepped out in faith. Though my husband was praying about this with me, he wasn't a true believer. He was obviously very open to accepting Christ, but he just hadn't fully committed himself yet."

For one year Josie and her husband prayed and tithed consistently. "We didn't understand it," she says, "but we knew God wanted to grow our confidence in Him. We were acting purely in faith, believing He would come through for us. And remember, this was still during the time my husband wasn't really a Christian."

Josie and her husband had three children, and she was a stay-at-home mom. "The first thing we did each month was pay the tithe on our $1,200 monthly check. We did everything we could to save money. We pulled back on eating out and tried our best to cut corners."

One day during that first year of tithing, Josie grabbed the mail from the mailbox. As she and her husband opened everything, they noticed that they'd received a check that neither was expecting. "It was in the amount of what we had tithed that year—plus an extra ten dollars," Josie says. "Oh, how we needed that money! And the timing was perfect.

"My husband was finished testing God. He gave his life to Christ, and we were baptized together! We knew that God was showing us His faithfulness and teaching us that He will always provide. From that moment on, we haven't stopped tithing and have never forgotten God's faithfulness. We lost money by giving it to Him, but we gained money back from Him when we gave. His ways are certainly not our ways, but we trust Him!"

Sometimes Christians say that tithing is only an Old Testament concept. The truth is that it's as necessary today as it was during the days of the Old Testament. Jesus actually carried the concept of tithing to the New Testament. Remember the story of the widow's mite (see Mark 12:41–44)? What a great lesson on tithing. The New Testament shows us that if Jesus is truly *Lord* of our lives, then *everything* we have belongs to Him!

When we fail to tithe, we're actually robbing God of what belongs to Him. If every Christian would simply tithe 10 percent to his or her church, no pastor would ever have to preach on money again! But statistics show us that only about 20 percent of a church's congregation tithe. The other 80 percent sometimes give an offering, but they're not tithers.[1]

When we tithe, we're showing God that we trust Him. When we give Him at least 10 percent of all we earn, we give God an opportunity to increase our confidence in Him!

I used to belong to a church in Colorado where the pastor preached on tithing one Sunday and encouraged those who weren't tithing to begin doing it. "Just step out in faith and do it," he said. "After three months, if God isn't meeting your needs, we'll return your tithe to you."

The underlying fact was that he *knew* God would meet our needs. Sometimes a Christian will say, "I don't agree with the way our church does things, so I'm not tithing to my church, but I will tithe to another ministry."

Yet the Bible clearly instructs us to give to the "storehouse"—our local church. If you want to give beyond God's tithe to another ministry, that's fine. But don't withhold from the church simply because you disagree with something. That would be like eating lunch at McDonald's but walking across the street to Burger King to pay your bill. Give your tithe where you're fed. And watch God increase your confidence in Him. What little is lost will soon be given back. He *will* meet your needs!

1. Melissa Steffan, "An Inside Look at Church Attenders Who Tithe the Most," *ChristianityToday.com*, May 17, 2013, www.christianitytoday.com/gleanings/2013/may/inside-look-at-church-attenders-who-tithe-most.html.

DAY 34

God Is My Husband (Part 1)

*"For your Maker is your husband—the Lord Almighty
is his name—the Holy One of Israel is your Redeemer;
he is called the God of all the earth."*
Isaiah 54:5

Nancy and Doug were high school sweethearts and had been married for thirty-five years when Doug developed Huntington's disease—a neurodegenerative genetic disorder that affects muscle coordination. It also leads to mental decline (often dementia) and behavioral symptoms such as jerky body movements and writhing.

"Our three children were grown and had families of their own," Nancy says. "Doug was a roofer by trade and began to lose his ability to get on a roof safely. My son worked with him and said he needed to stop working because he was no longer safe."

Up to that time, Doug had crashed five motorcycles. He lost his license. So now Doug could no longer ride a cycle, drive a car, or work. He couldn't use the telephone any longer because he was unable to operate a smartphone.

"Times were hard," Nancy says, "but our faith was strong." Doug and Nancy had both made commitments to Christ early in their lives and knew His faithfulness firsthand.

After a year, Nancy and Doug's savings were almost gone. "I still had confidence in God, however, that He was in control and was going to take care of us," Nancy says. "I contacted the Social Security Administration to see if Doug was eligible for Medicare. It was a relief to discover that he qualified. I worked very hard to lower our bills and to get some financial relief."

During this same time, Nancy's parents were aging and needed assistance. After praying about it and engaging in lots of dialogue, they moved in with Doug and Nancy. "It was such a relief to have them here to help me some with Doug," Nancy says. "And I just needed someone to talk to! Doug was still making verbal sounds, but it was usually impossible to understand him. He and my mom became very close friends."

It was also during this time that Nancy discovered she had large granular lymphocytic (LGL for short) leukemia. She didn't share this news with many people, though, because she didn't want them to worry about her, and because she felt her husband was the one who needed the most attention.

"My boat was being tossed about," Nancy says, "but my lifeguard walks on water, and my God confidence remained strong. I knew He would protect me."

In January 2014, Nancy's mother passed away. "She was in my dad's arms here at the house," Nancy says. "This was devastating to Doug. It was for me, too, but because I was so sick, it was difficult to grieve with him.

"I'm an only child, and my mom and I were best friends. I took her to many doctor's appointments. We had some amazing heart-to-heart talks through the years. Right before she died, she became very confused, but I was able to pray with her and reassure her that she was going to heaven. Both my parents have always exhibited strong relationships with Christ. My God confidence was strong. I had no doubt where she was going."

About five months later, Nancy's LGL leukemia began causing extreme anemia problems. She had an appointment with the oncologist for a blood transfusion, but when she arrived at the doctor's office, she had a temperature of 102.8, so they were unable to do the transfusion.

Nancy was admitted to the hospital, and while she was there the doctor discovered that she had pneumonia. "I guess I was where I needed to be," Nancy says. "God knew. I had given all I had to my family at home, and I now had nothing left to give."

DAY 35

God Is My Husband (Part 2)

After you have suffered a little while, our God, who is full
of kindness through Christ, will give you his eternal glory.
He personally will come and pick you up, and set you
firmly in place, and make you stronger than ever.
1 PETER 5:10 TLB

Nancy's sister-in-law was visiting from out of town and was able to help around the house for a short time while Nancy was hospitalized, and Nancy's youngest daughter was able to help as well. "I was amazed with my daughter! She was caring for us, caring for her own family, working a full-time job, and also serving as a youth pastor's wife. Her plate was more than full!"

Nancy's sister-in-law arranged for outside help for Doug so Nancy could work on regaining her own strength. Home health care arrived and made a big difference, but they were only able to stay a short while. After that, Nancy knew it would be up to her again to meet the needs of her father and husband.

Doug was now unable to eat. He couldn't swallow food or liquids. "He had lost so much weight," Nancy says, "that he was literally skin and bones. It was remarkable to me that he was able to walk short distances—from the couch to the kitchen, et cetera."

As Doug's decline continued, hospice was enlisted. "For months Doug had been saying the same thing to me over and over," Nancy remembers. "It was very difficult to understand him, but I'm certain he was telling me that he no longer wanted to be here and was ready for heaven. I understood why he would feel that way. My God confidence continued to grow. I knew heaven was ahead."

Even though Nancy didn't want it to happen, it did. The love of her life passed away. Hospice had been in the home for three weeks. They did all they could to make Doug comfortable. "The hospice nurse explained that terminally ill people often become almost impossible to comfort right before they die. Doug couldn't remain comfortable for more than three minutes at a time. He was uncontrollably restless."

Nancy was still having difficulty recovering from the pneumonia. Her children and friends from the church were able to stop by with food and offered what care they could give, but there just wasn't much that could be done at this point.

"Doug got up from his chair and went to the kitchen table for three bites of mashed potatoes that a church friend had brought," Nancy says. "He then pushed himself away from the table, stretched out on the couch, got as comfortable as he could, convulsed quietly three times, and then stopped breathing. He was finally where he wanted to be."

In her mind, Nancy could see her husband running into his Savior's arms free from pain and disability. She and Doug had been married for almost forty years.

"It hasn't been easy," she says, "but God is still on the throne! My faith remains strong, and God continues to care for my dad and me. God has promised to be my husband."

And Nancy's LGL leukemia? That part of the story hasn't ended yet. Nancy continues to take oral medication three times a day. She has her blood drawn every three weeks and is scheduled to see her doctor every three months. "I feel better than I did a year ago," Nancy says. "And I'm still trusting God to heal me. My confidence in Him just keeps getting stronger and stronger. He *will* heal me—either here on earth or in heaven. I praise Him for His faithfulness!"

When life falls apart, your loved ones pass away, your own health is in question, and you don't know what the future holds, rely on 1 John 5:13. You can have God confidence in the things that can never be taken from you! Your relationship with Him can remain strong. Your faith can continue to grow. And you can rest assured that He really is in control.

GOD CONFIDENCE IN A VARIETY OF SITUATIONS

DAY 36

A Light at the End of a Very Dark Tunnel

But I trust in you, LORD; I say, "You are my God."
PSALM 31:14

Pastor Chad had been through a difficult year. His wife had been spending an exorbitant amount of time with a friend from work. He was concerned because even though the woman was nice, she wasn't a Christ follower. She didn't share their values or morality.

"I had hoped my wife and I would be a strong ministry team," Chad says. "But she seemed disillusioned about ministry and had mentioned that she didn't like being a pastor's wife. Though my ministry was going great, our marriage began to suffer."

Only eight months into their pastorate, Chad's wife accepted a position in a department store back in the city they had moved from to pastor their current church. "Because finances were tight, we had agreed that she'd look for work," he says. "But I naturally assumed it would be locally!"

Chad hurt for his church family. He knew it wasn't fair that they were losing their pastor after only nine months, but he also knew he wanted his marriage to survive. So he resigned and they moved. "It was during this time that I discovered my wife was having inappropriate conversations with another man. She confessed to me that she had met him for one night."

Chad was crushed. *Was it something I did? Something I said?* he wondered. "She simply told me that she didn't love me anymore and that we were only together out of obligation."

Besides being afraid of losing his marriage and their four children, Chad was also genuinely concerned about his wife's spiritual state. "I didn't want her to lose her soul because she didn't enjoy being in ministry with me," he says.

Chad's God confidence was strong. He knew God was *for* marriage. "God gave me the ability to forgive her," he says. "I embraced her and thought we were on a road to reconciliation."

That belief was short-lived. Within weeks, Chad discovered that his wife was involved with another man—a younger man. "I felt so emasculated. I asked her what she wanted from me. I was willing to do whatever it would take to keep our marriage together. She told me she loved me and wanted our marriage to work."

Chad's wife told him they weren't connecting emotionally anymore, so he suggested they go to counseling. "I *wanted* to be connected emotionally with my wife again," he says. "But unfortunately, she didn't want to abide by the boundaries expressed by our pastor and other counselors. She continued to see the younger man."

Chad was in constant conversation with God. "I asked Him 'Why?' a lot. I knew He wouldn't usurp my wife's free will, but I so wanted Him to remove all obstacles to save my family. When she filed for divorce, I just wanted God to take me to heaven.

"I refused to entertain suicidal thoughts, and I was still confident that God would keep working in my life. I'm a man of faith. I've always known that nothing is beyond God's grace. So I submitted myself to the leading and support of my senior pastor. He told me what I needed to hear, not what I wanted to hear. He became a sounding board for me as well as a source of accountability."

Chad made a pledge to God: "You may never bless me beyond where I am now, and I may never meet another woman with whom to share my life, but I will never deny You." He also prayed Psalm 102 every day.

"Our divorce was final six months later. We got joint custody of our four children, and they continued to go to church with me. My children witnessed their mother moving on with her life, and I tried to move along with mine. Divorce is hell. With all that the kids and I had experienced, I resolved to be the best dad I could be and let God take care of my desire to grow old with someone."

Little did Chad know that God would bless him much

sooner than he could imagine. He crossed paths with a former coworker who used to serve as children's pastor at the same church he served as associate pastor. "She has never been married, and her only children are those she has pastored. It was definitely a God thing," Chad says.

Alison had been commissioned to serve as a missionary in New Zealand by her and Chad's denomination. She was pastoring the church in Whangarei and was simply home for deputation. But during that time, she and Chad sparked a special friendship and she promised to continue communicating with him as she returned to New Zealand.

"After a few months of e-mails and Skype conversations, I confessed that I had developed feelings for her. She shared the same. Now I pray Psalm 105 frequently."

Chad and Alison will be married in February 2016 back in the States and will serve on staff at the same church in which they had originally served together.

"God answered my prayers when I didn't know how to pray," Chad says. "His faithfulness is constant. Our faithfulness rests on our choices. I'm learning to choose God confidence on a moment-by-moment basis."

DAY 37

Only God Can Help Me with This!

Cast your cares on the LORD and he will sustain you;
he will never let the righteous be shaken.
PSALM 55:22

In the past three years, Cindy has experienced more than her share of sorrow. "My grandmother, mother, husband, and father have all died," she says. "And I've had four surgeries in a year—one surgery because of cancer. I went through radiation, and thankfully, my cancer was caught early."

Cindy's physician has told her that the cancer won't kill her. People often ask her how she's coped with so much sorrow. She even lost her home due to medical bills from her husband's illness. "I'm now living in my parents' home," she says. "I know I couldn't have endured any of this without Christ. He has given me more confidence in Him than I ever imagined possible."

—

Kerri moved from one state to another in 2007—right at the time when houses weren't selling and the economy had dipped. She decided to rent her house, and a wonderful couple moved in. "I packed up and left the state without a worry," she says. "After all, I had wonderful people renting my house, and I was excited about my new start in another state."

Kerri quickly settled into her new apartment and job. But after being there for only one month, she received a call from her renters informing her they were going to have to leave without proper notice. "They said they'd be out in two months," Kerri recalls.

Kerri's God confidence kicked into high gear. "I have a solid relationship with Christ, and He has always met my needs," she says. "I didn't know how it would work out, but I knew that God cared about every single detail of my life—including my house being rented."

Kerri immediately put her house on the market, and in spite of the economy, it sold right away. "I never had to make two house payments," she said. "God never ceases to amaze me!"

—

Mindy has been a nurse for years, and she has also spent time on the mission field. "I love taking care of people, and I'm crazy about God," she says. "So missions and nursing just go hand in hand for me."

Though Mindy has enjoyed serving in a variety of countries, she knows she's also a missionary right here in the United States. "I've always had a lot of God confidence," she says. "But for twenty years I flew in a medical helicopter picking up severely injured and sick people and treating them."

On two different calls, Mindy experienced something

she'll never forget. "I had the privilege of seeing someone's soul leave his body and go heavenward. On one of the occasions, my medical partner and the pilot—who are both Christians—saw this happen as well."

Many hospice nurses share stories of seeing Christians in their last few moments reaching up with their eyes fixed on something. Families who have witnessed their loved ones do this at passing believe they're seeing Jesus and His angels beckoning them to heaven.

Hospice nurses will also share that those who aren't Christians and who are awake as they're slipping from life will often grimace and pull back—as if they're trying not to be taken somewhere. Nurses have also testified to the smell of fire and sulphur when an unbeliever winces as he dies. They often believe this is the sign of a non-Christian who's beginning to experience the fringes of hell.

Mindy's God confidence increased even more as witnessed the eternal passing from one state of life to a "I'm so confident in Christ," she says. "There's just in me that He is always in control. I'm only ther hands and feet. Ultimately, He is the true Heal tumor.

Paula just found out last October that she od say, 'You "My husband, I myself, and a friend all —the kind that *are going to be okay.'* I had a deep, settle ys. only He can give—the entire time,"

Paula was sent to a variety of doctors and had different tests run. "Even on the very day of my surgery, I had God's peace," she recalls.

The result: no chemo or radiation was needed. "This is almost unheard of for someone like me who's over sixty," she says. The third MRI was taken the day before her surgery, and it showed that the tumor was smaller and had moved away from her motor strip. Had it not moved, the surgery would have been much more dangerous.

"God confidence? He gives plenty of it if we'll simply ask," Paula says.

DAY 38

Just in Time

*"Peace I leave with you; my peace I give you.
I do not give to you as the world gives. Do not
let your hearts be troubled and do not be afraid."*
JOHN 14:27

Jamie and her husband love having their three adult sons home for holidays. "Two of our boys live in the same state as we do, but our middle son lives on the East Coast," she says. "Holidays have always been a special family time—especially Christmas. We love to read the Christmas story from Luke, spend time in prayer, and just enjoy one another's company as we share gifts."

When her middle son, Lee, was in college and on the East Coast, Jamie realized she and her husband didn't have the money to fly him home for Christmas. "Even though I had spent the morning searching online for an airline ticket, the prices were extremely high, and my heart sank when I realized it was out of our control. How could we enjoy Christmas without all three boys here with us?"

She also knew his campus would close for the holidays. Though he could remain in his dorm, he'd be without food unless he braved the cold weather and walked a few miles to the nearest restaurant.

"I began praying immediately," Jamie says. "God has always been the center of our home, and my husband prays on his knees every night before climbing into bed. We've seen God do more for us than I could ever explain."

After praying about the matter, Jamie was suddenly overwhelmed with a deep peace. "I knew immediately it was the Lord," she says. "He seemed to say, *'Trust Me. Just trust Me.'*"

Jamie continued her workday with a lightened heart and increased God confidence. "I actually stopped thinking and worrying about it," she says.

When she got home after work, she noticed the message light blinking on their answering machine. "I wept as I listened to the message from a dear friend," Jamie says.

"Hey, Jamie. It's Shelley. I'm flying from Chicago to Cincinnati today, and my Chicago flight is full. They asked for volunteers to take a later flight. For some reason, Lee popped into my mind. I don't know if you've already purchased an airline ticket for him to come home for Christmas, but by waiting here a few more hours in Chicago and taking a later flight, I'm getting a voucher good for a round-trip ticket anywhere in the States. I'll send it to you to make sure Lee gets home for Christmas. Love you!"

"I believed it, but I couldn't believe it," Jamie says. "Yes, I had God confidence that He was going to take care of the matter, but I had no idea it would come this quickly or be this easy. And I knew Shelley loved to travel. She could have easily used that voucher on a vacation for herself. But God was moving! He worked in *my* life to teach me not to worry and that He cares about bringing my boys home. And He also moved in Shelley's life to bring my son to her mind."

When Jamie and her husband picked up their son at the airport, he was running a fever and had a severe case of strep throat. "We went straight from the airport to the emergency room," she says. "He spent the entire Christmas break in bed recuperating, but I had the privilege of caring for him as only a mom can.

"I shudder to think of the possibility of him being alone in a big dorm without medicine, running a fever, no access to a nurse, no car. God is certainly in the business of caring for His children."

Lee needed to be home that Christmas—maybe just to get well—and God made sure it happened.

But the story doesn't end here.

The following Christmas, Lee had an airline ticket and flew home for the holidays, and when his parents picked him up at the airport, he was sick again. "This particular year," Jamie says, "there was an outbreak of meningitis among college students around the nation."

He flew in with a temperature of 104 degrees, and again they drove straight to the emergency room. "The doctor performed a spinal tap on Lee and was then done with his shift. But instead of going home," Jamie says, "he decided to stay and wait for the results.

"I'll never forget the doctor's words. 'This isn't a matter of *if* he has meningitis—it's a matter of whether it's bacterial or viral meningitis.' "

Jamie and her husband were numb. Yet rising from deep within their hearts, they felt the familiar God confidence fueling itself into flame. "We began praying immediately. Our extended families prayed, and our friends prayed."

The results from the spinal tap were back, and the doctor stared closely at them. "We felt as though our hearts were pounding through our chests," Jamie says.

"I'm really surprised at this," the doctor stated. "It's not viral *or* bacterial. Your son doesn't have meningitis at all! I just don't understand."

It was Christmas Eve. Lee's fever broke immediately. Once again he was home for the holidays with his own God confidence to share. God *is* in control. Of tests. Of test results. Of fevers. And even of airline tickets.

DAY 39

Sympathy or Symphony?

*"I therefore looked for good to come. Evil came instead.
I waited for the light. Darkness came. My heart is troubled
and restless. Waves of affliction have come upon me."*
JOB 30:26–27 TLB

*"We cannot imagine the power of the Almighty, and yet
he is so just and merciful that he does not destroy us."*
JOB 37:23 TLB

Kristine had taken her son from their home in California to her parents' house in Colorado so he could spend some time with his grandparents. "I had only been on the road for a few hours when my dad called and told me that Mom was in the hospital. She seemed fine when I hugged her good-bye," Kristine says. "I asked Dad if I should return, but he told me to keep going home; he simply wanted to keep me in the loop."

Twelve hours later, Kristine's dad called again and pleaded with her to get back to Colorado as quickly as she could. Her mom had taken a fast decline for the worse.

Kristine remembers feeling scared, anxious, numb, sad, and confused. She immediately started praying as she began the thirteen-hour drive to her parents' home. "I asked God to show Himself to me," she says. "And as soon as those words left my mouth, I had such a great peace."

By the time she arrived in Colorado, things were even worse. "My mom had suffered an aortic dissection, and there was little chance for recovery," Kristine says. "I knew God was there with us. His presence was so close! My confidence in Him assured me that whatever happened, He was going to use this for His glory."

Kristine's mom passed away three days later. At her funeral service, several people shared how she was instrumental in causing God to work in their lives. "We eventually went back to our normal routines," Kristine says. "But I knew God wasn't finished using my mom's life."

Three years later, Kristine's younger brother gave his life to Christ. "Our family had been praying for more than twenty years for his salvation. Because he saw the faith that I had and the fact that I trusted God in this painful situation, he knew he wanted what I had. God really does have the power to use all things for His glory."

Now Kristine's brother also lives with strong God confidence and leans on it often.

It's been said that when bad things happen to us, we can either recruit *sympathy* or demonstrate a *symphony*. A Christian who lacks God confidence relishes sympathy. Because his faith is weak, he depends on the sympathy and attention from others to make him feel better.

But a Christian who lives with God confidence produces a symphony in the midst of hard times. Using the pain, he learns to orchestrate beautiful music out of the situation. He grows from it. He learns how to become even stronger in his faith. And to those around him, he's a witness of God's harmony and peace.

He doesn't need to feed his ego by enlisting sympathy and attention from those around him; instead, he uses his pain to minister to those who watch his life. What a symphony of God's grace!

Think about Job from the Old Testament. He certainly had his share of grief and loss! He was a wealthy man who lost his entire family and all his livestock in one day. Instead of calling attention to himself, he sought God. When his friends came to visit, they tried to convince him he had sinned and brought the calamities on himself.

Still Job didn't recruit sympathy from them—though they were willing to give it if he would admit his sin. Job knew he was righteous. He was packed with God confidence. He knew that bad things happened both to good people and to bad people.

He patiently waited on God, and his Creator used Job's life to create a symphony of His mercy. God gave Job back several times what he had lost. What a symphony of God's love!

DAY 40
True Forgiveness

Bear with each other and forgive one another if any of you has a grievance against someone. Forgive as the Lord forgave you.
COLOSSIANS 3:13

Elaine's dad died recently. He was a predatory pedophile who was addicted to pornography. "He was also an unfaithful husband and a very angry man," Elaine says. "Others, though, saw him as compassionate, giving, and very quiet. I guess it depended on what part of his life you were in. When he went to jail many years ago, several people didn't believe he had done the things for which he was convicted. That's how masking, conniving, and manipulative his behavior was."

When Elaine was struggling with forgiveness, God showed her that Christ asked God to forgive people *as they were in the process* of killing Him. "At that point, God challenged me," she says. "Could I forgive my dad while he was in the process of abusing someone—because of the phrase Christ prayed from the cross: 'They don't know what they're doing'?"

Elaine believed that if her dad were in his right mind, he never would have done the sinful things he did. "I began to believe if Dad could see himself standing before God and could view the truth of all the ripple effects of damage he created—before he did them—he wouldn't have done those things."

Elaine's dad struggled with mental illness. Her family believes he was abused during his childhood. "This doesn't excuse his actions," she says, "but it helps explain them. It enables us to understand a tiny bit of why he turned out the way he did."

Elaine and her brother had experienced hard and challenging lives trying to overcome their past and learning to trust their heavenly Father. God confidence has been difficult for them.

"But God is faithful," she says. "We have learned to forgive the man who hurt so many people. We even prayed that God would have mercy on his soul. Eternity is a long time to spend in hell.

"Many people expect Christians to forgive and to forget," Elaine says. "But this is faulty thinking. Our history becomes part of our testimony and a powerful witness of the grace and mercy of almighty God.

"Forgiveness is extended when we're no longer holding grudges against others. With God's help, we can actually desire complete healing and spiritual restoration for those who have hurt us."

When we learn to forgive as Christ forgives, God confidence is the natural by-product.

Is there someone in your life to whom you need to extend

forgiveness? Take some time right now to ask God to bring to your mind anyone whom you haven't forgiven.

Holding a grudge will create bitterness inside your heart, and it will also make your God confidence impossible. You can't live with genuine faith in Him if you're unforgiving and angry toward someone who has hurt you.

By refusing to forgive those who have hurt us, we limit God's action in our lives. He chooses to forgive *us* when we choose to forgive *others*. We may not immediately *feel* as though we have forgiven someone, but forgiveness isn't a feeling; it's a decision.

Begin to pray, "Dear God, I choose to forgive. I'm deciding right now to forgive. Please help my feelings to eventually match my words."

You can trust God. He's big enough to do that.

BONUS DAY 41
Does God Like Mexican Food?

"You keep him in perfect peace whose mind is
stayed on you, because he trusts in you."
ISAIAH 26:3 ESV

Abbie had ridden the bus alone to First Church almost every Sunday since she was a little girl. Now, at seventeen, her attendance was sporadic. "She had a troubled past," Sherri says. "Her home life was terrible. She had recently been kicked out of her home, and she had moved in with a friend."

Sherri and Abbie were friends on Facebook, and Sherri noticed that she kept remarking about how much she missed her mom's tamales. Because Sherri had given Abbie so much attention at church during the years, she felt as though she were a second mom to her.

"I had been her coach on our Bible quizzing team, and I taught the Bible study she was in on Wednesday evenings," Sherri said. "I was just very involved in her life. I truly cared about her, and I missed her not being at church every week."

It had been about six months since Abbie had been to church when God told Sherri to take her two plates of tamales. "But God," Sherri said, "I only have twelve dollars left until I get paid, and I still need to feed my family this evening."

Sherri didn't know where she'd find the money for

groceries if she spent money on tamales, but God's message was extremely clear. "I've heard Him speak before," she says. "And I've learned through the years that even when I don't understand *how* He will come through, my confidence in Him remains strong that He *will* come through."

After getting off work, Sherri was exhausted and wanted to go home and begin dinner for her family, but God's voice reminded her of the two plates of tamales she needed to take to Abbie and her friend.

"I drove to the closest Mexican food restaurant and went to the drive-through, placing my order for two plates of tamales," she said.

"We're all out of tamales," the employee informed her. *Seriously?* she thought. Sherri began to dismiss the tamale thing as a bad idea and started home. But she had barely driven down the block before she heard God's voice again, *"Two plates of tamales."*

So she drove to the next Mexican restaurant and repeated her order. She couldn't believe it when she was told they didn't have any tamales. *You're kidding me!* she couldn't help but think.

She headed to the third Mexican restaurant, ordered two plates of tamales, and waited for thirty minutes to get them. "It took all the money I had," Sherri says. "I then drove to the girls' house and rang the doorbell." Tamale delivery completed!

When she arrived home, she was hounded with questions from her family about why she was so late, and what they were having for dinner, among other questions. "I didn't tell them where I'd been or what I had done," Sherri said.

Her husband showed her the mail and handed her a letter that had come for her. "I opened it and found an unexpected check for a little more than one thousand dollars!"

God confidence? Absolutely!

"I hadn't met Abbie's friend until I delivered the tamales to their house that day," Sherri says. "Later Abbie called to thank me and shared that her friend was having suicidal thoughts. Abbie didn't know who to talk to or how to help her, but my delivery of tamales reminded her that I cared and that we could pray together for God's salvation in her friend's life."

God is good. All the time.

All the time. God is good.

About the Author

Susie Shellenberger is a full-time speaker and author who travels forty-two weeks/weekends every year speaking to a variety of audiences in churches, camps, and conferences. She loves to eat cereal for dinner, has written fifty-four books, and is an OKC Thunder basketball fan (she has given the invocation at four of their games). She lives in Bethany, Oklahoma, with her two miniature schnauzers, Obie and Amos, and can sometimes be seen taking them for rides in the basket of her three-wheeled bicycle.

Notes

Notes

Notes

Notes

Notes

Notes

Notes

Notes

Also available from goTandem

gotandemresources.com